ANGELS

ANGELS
MESSENGERS OF THE DIVINE

FLORA MACALLAN

Bath · New York · Singapore · Hong Kong · Cologne · Delhi · Melbourne

CONTENTS

This edition published in 2010

Copyright © Parragon Books Ltd
Queen Street House
4 Queen Street
Bath BA1, 1 HE, UK

Original edition: ditter. projektagentur GmbH
Project coordination and picture research:
   Irina Ditter-Hilkens
Series design: Claudio Martinez
Layout and typesetting: Burga Fillery

English edition produced by: APE Int'l., LLC
Translation: Russell Cennydd, Christine Yoshida

ISBN: 978-1-4054-9176-1
Printed in Indonesia

The Hierarchy of Angels 34

The Dark Side of Angels 58

Additional Concepts of Angels 72

Keanu Reeves in *Constantine,* a supernatural thriller in which the Archangel Gabriel has joined forced with the Devil.

ANGELS ARE OMNIPRESENT

While the existence of angels may be a matter of belief, they are nonetheless pervasive in today's culture. Angels feature not only at Christmastime, when they are sung about, printed onto gift wrapping, and crown the Christmas tree; they are found in every other season and throughout popular culture, in literature, music, cinema, and theater.

The repertoire of the Irish band U2 includes the song *Angel of Harlem,* the English band Depêche Mode named one of its albums *Playing The Angel,* and the American band Faith No More chose the title *Angel Dust.* Angels have long been common motifs for artists of all kinds, usually without having any particular knowledge of their nature. The advertising industry also takes advantage of the angel, especially the guardian angel, in order to extol a particularly safe

product or service. In Germany, for example, the slogan *"Never drive faster than your guardian angel can fly"* was used to urge drivers to stick to an appropriate speed.

Angels in Hollywood

The Hollywood dream industry has long known the powerful draw of angels, as well. In the film *City of Angels,* starring Nicolas Cage and Meg Ryan, the angel Seth falls in love with Dr. Maggie Rice and renounces his immortality for her. John Travolta plays the Archangel of the same name in the film *Michael,* and in *The Preacher's Wife,* Oscar Award winner Denzel Washington plays an angel with an important role to

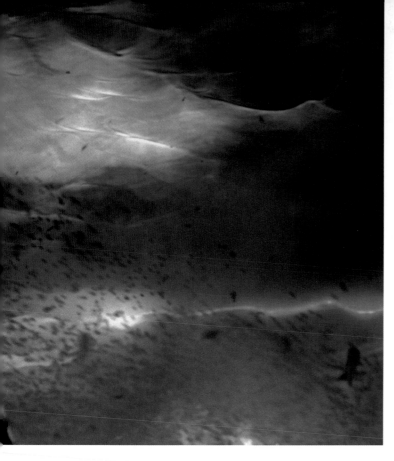

Maria Rilke—and by no means always in religious or Christian settings. Painters have taken up the theme of angels in every time period, including Mark Chagall, Paul Klee, Lovis Corinth, and Max Beckmann, to mention only a few twentieth-century artists. It would be difficult to find the museum that didn't include some representations of angels.

Longing for spirituality

The ubiquity of angels may be an indication that many people, regardless of their faith in God or a church, believe in the existence of a personal guardian angel who looks out for them. In recent years, there seems to be a resurgence of longing for spirituality, which has renewed interest in the nature of angels. In today's progress-oriented world, driven as it is by technological and scientific thought, angels take on new meaning.

play on earth. The angel thriller *The Prophecy* (released as *God's Army: The Last Battle* in Europe) was so successful that four sequels were made. In the first film, the Archangel Gabriel starts a rebellion because he is jealous of God's special love for humans. The director of the film *Constantine* (featuring *Matrix* star Keanu Reeves) also found inspiration in this theme. His villainous Archangel Gabriel is played by a woman—which has a sound basis in mythology (see page 50).

One Archangel that is familiar especially in Judaism has enjoyed a particularly successful career. In the film *Dogma*, Metatron was represented—as the voice of God—by Alan Rickman. He is also found in the fantasy novel *Good Omens* by Terry Pratchett and Neil Gaiman, and again in Philip Pullman's trilogy *His Dark Materials*. This Archangel even appears in the Japanese anime series *Angel Sanctuary*. Angels are to be found in the work of many internationally renowned literary figures, such as Franz Kafka, Max Frisch, or Rainer

Angels are everywhere, even on the catwalks of the great fashion metropolises. This winged spirit is not a heavenly, divine messenger, but a model.

American psychologist Julian Jaynes believes that divine voices could once communicate with humans through the right brain. Today their messages can only reach us in the form of notions, intuitions and visions.

The extraordinary magnitude of the angelic realm is connected with the fact that early in Christianity, as in Judaism, pagan gods and nature spirits replaced by the new tradition found their way into the relevant religious worlds as angels. Among other things, this was one means of making it easier for those who believed in them to change to the new religious system.

Heaven, Earth, and Hell

Although spiritual beings of various kinds are found in many, but not all, religions, the classical kind of angel occurs only in the three monotheistic religions, which are those grounded in belief in a single God. These are Judaism, Islam, and Christianity. Hinduism and Buddhism, which are both likewise great world religions, know no angels.

The three-tiered cosmos, consisting of Heaven, Earth, and Hell, is common to Judaism and its descendants,

Conflicting sources

The realm of angels is extremely complex; and there is not just a single Heaven, but several. These Heavens are populated with no fewer than ten heavenly choirs (or orders) of angels. There are well-known Archangels, and the available sources are not in agreement about them. Sometimes it is even unclear whether an angel is aligned with the forces of good or those of evil.

Texts frequently contradict each other as to the nature of angels, their tasks, their names, and the most important angel appearances. The Apocryphal texts (see box on page 9) serve as our primary source of information about them, since they discuss the divine and infernal realms in the greatest detail.

Most religions believe in a three-tiered cosmos, and it tends to be represented as in this picture: the human world lies between Heaven (the realm of God and the angels) and Hell (the realm of the Devil and demons).

The Apocrypha

Nearly all of the relatively precise information about angels comes from texts that are no longer to be found among the canonical works of Judaism, Islam, and Christianity. Anyone wanting to know about the angels in detail must search for it in "secret" texts: the heretical, pseudoepigraphical, or apocryphal sources. In this respect, the Book of Enoch (Ethiopian, Slavic, and Hebrew Book of Enoch) is one of the most important sources for angel research. Some of these sources were originally included in the accepted canon, and parts were even important and acknowledged sources. Later, however, they were judged to be noncanonical. The reason for this was usually that they no longer corresponded to the worldview of current religious dogma. At the Council of Trent (1545–1563, called the Tridentine period), among others, The Catholic Church established which books belonged to the canon of the Christian Bible.

A few books of the Apocrypha, however, belong to the canon according to some Christian churches but not in others.

The Council of Trent determined which books belong to the Bible.

Islam and Christianity. Heaven is the realm of the angels, and Hell the place farthest from the God of the Old Testament, where the Devil resides. But both sides are present and become active in the middle tier: Earth.

The realm of the angels and demons is incredibly complex and fascinating. It is also full of contradictions, and resistant to scientific explanation. Whether or not an individual believes in angels—and if so, in which ones and in what model of Heaven—is purely a matter of faith.

In contemporary science, there are indeed a number of reports and scholarly work that support the existence of angelic spiritual beings. The American psychologist Julian Jaynes, for example, set out a daring thesis about them in his book *The Origin of Consciousness in the Breakdown of the Bicameral Mind*. As is well-known, the left half of the human brain is responsible for language and rationality, while the right balances this with intuition, fantasy, creativity, and emotion. Today, in Jaynes' opinion, the left side is used substantially more than the right. The right side remains underdeveloped, and therefore remains silent.

Yet, according to Jaynes, this is precisely the part of our brain that has the potential to perceive the divine. Originally, the right brain was receptive to and obeyed only divine intuitions, but modern humans have largely lost that ability. In its place, approximately 3,000 years ago, the right brain developed consciousness. But the heavenly connection is not completely vanquished: in hunches, intuitions, and visions it is still effective today. And humans have a deep-seated yearning for spirituality that supports his thesis. Jaynes cites this yearning to explain the great contemporary interest in angels.

Jaynes' theories have only found limited favor, and in some respects are extremely dubious. But the thought that people in earlier ages had a more direct connection with the divine, and that this condition could theoretically be recovered, is also at the heart of many New Age movements. In these, too, angels are seen as intermediaries with the divine.

The Realm of
Angels

According to the Bible, the Israelites fed on manna during their sojourn in the desert, which God caused to rain from Heaven—is this the angels' food?

THE FOOD OF THE ANGELS

The issue of angels' need for food depends on whether they are seen as purely spiritual beings or as material forms. If the first is the case, it may be assumed that angels either have no need for food or, perhaps, that their food is utterly different from that of humans. Today most theologians assume that angels, as spiritual beings, do not take in food in the classical sense, but feed on "the sight of God."

This possibility is supported by a passage in the Book of Tobit, also called the Book of Tobias (12:19), in which the Archangel Raphael says, "All these days I merely appeared to you and did not eat or drink, but you were seeing a vision."

Legend has it that Catherine of Siena, shown with Saint Dominick in the painting on the right, ate only communion wafers, which are called "the bread of angels."

Hildegard of Bingen

The nun, monastery founder and abbess Hildegard of Bingen is considered the greatest of all the German mystics. She was born in the state of Hessen in 1098, and died in the town of Bingen on the Rhine in 1179. She had divine visions from her childhood, which she started writing down in Latin after 1141. She was an accomplished scholar, healer, poet, composer of music, and the author of theological texts, and in addition to all of that, a dedicated reformer of church life. These days, she is particularly well-known for her faith healing work. During her lifetime she catalogued some 280 plants and trees according to their healing properties.

A folio from Hildegard of Bingen's *Liber divinorum operum*. Shown here is the image of the *Universal Man*.

According to Hildegard of Bingen, on the other hand, angels nourish themselves with a substance similar to morning dew, which dissolves automatically.

Psalm 78:24–25 contains a passage about God sustaining the Israelites during their desert migration. It describes how the Lord "rained down upon them manna to eat, and gave them the grain of Heaven. Man ate of the bread of the angels..." This "bread of the angels" (also called the "bread of the mighty" in many translations), manna, is definitely not invisible, but instead can be seen and consumed by people. It is also described as white and sugar-like. According to Exodus (16:13-14), it fell with the morning dew, and any surplus would vanish in the heat of the sun (Ex 16:21) as the day progressed.

Aphid honeydew

Some scientists believe Biblical manna is a secretion of aphids or scale insects, as these produce a white liquid with a high sugar content that usually occurs in a crystallized state. Older attempts to explain Biblical manna in scientific terms see it as the manna lichen (also known as desert lichen, *Sphaerothallia esculenta*), which is widespread in the Near East.

The bread of angels

Another theory connects the Host with the "bread of the angels." The Host, administered in the Christian sacrament of communion in the Orthodox and Reformed Churches, is a small disc-shaped wafer of unleavened flour dough. In old Latin, this word designated a sacrifice.

Ever since the thirteenth century, there have been stories of young women who limited their food intake entirely to the "bread of angels," in order to draw closer to Jesus. The most famous of these women is Saint Catherine of Siena (1347–1380), an Italian mystic and church teacher who died at just 33 years of age. Her goal was to become a terrestrial angel, and so for many long years she ate nothing but communion wafers. This diet may have contributed in part to her ability to attain a state of transcendental consciousness and to have visions. It is said that her soul often reached such a state of union with God that she hardly knew whether she was inside or outside her body.

ANGELS' GENDER

Angels are generally seen as sexless entities, neither male nor female, and without sexuality.

For the Catholic Church as in Judaism, angels are purely spiritual, sexless creatures. Sexuality is meaningless in relation to angels, since it is premised on the human body. Hence the statement in rabbinical literature that "In the world to come there is neither eating nor drinking, nor marrying…"

According to the patriarch Enoch, however, angels certainly can reproduce. In the thirteenth century, the Catholic Church, faced with sources that described angels as having sexual intercourse with human women (Genesis 6:1), came up with the "Grigori," the tenth choir of angels (see page 46). The visionary Emanuel Swedenborg (see page 74 ff) also gave detailed descriptions of the sex of the angels. By his explanation, there are indeed male and female angels: since angels were once human, after all, their sex corresponds to what it had been in their human state. Furthermore, male and female angels can apparently fuse to become sexless angels in Heaven.

Angels' wings
In images of angels, the shape of their wings is often based on that of great birds, particularly swans, geese or eagles. In his highly detailed book *Angels—An Endangered Species*, Malcolm Godwin maintains that no winged angels could ever fly—or at least, not in purely physical terms. At best, they would need special divine abilities to get off the ground. If angels were made of flesh and bone, they would weigh close to 200 pounds (about 90 kg), and would need a wingspan of 12 to 40 yards in order to fly—the equivalent of a hang glider. However, in the classic Renaissance image, their wingspan amounts to about 2 yards in relation to the body.

The Greek god of love, Cupid (or Eros), is depicted with wings and a bow, and served as a model for early depictions of angels.

ANGELS IN ART

Representations of winged spirits and divine messengers are found in the art of many ancient civilizations, from Sumerian and Babylonian to the Egyptian, Greek and Roman, to name only a few.

A wall painting dating to the second century AD in the Catacomb of Priscilla, Rome, is believed to be the earliest surviving image of an angel. Other famous early representations of angels include one in a grave near the Via Appia and another on an ivory plaque from the Martin von Reider collection in the Bavarian National Museum, Munich, both originating from the fourth century. In both images, the angels are clothed in a white tunic with toga. The angels are not barefoot, but wear sandals. The significant aspect of these representations is that the angels have no wings.

From Greek gods to angels

Representations of angels with wings go back to the fifth century. But the Bible mentions wings only in connection with the two highest choirs of angels (see page 40 ff). In art, wings differentiate angels from humans, and represent their ability to appear in the sky—as well as the fact that they are neither bound by the force of gravity nor limited to human speeds.

The golden age of angel imagery began in the eighth century. At that time, artists looked especially to Greek models for inspiration—notably to Nike, the Greek goddess of victory, who (apart from a single questionable exception) is always winged. The Greek god of love, who is the winged Cupid or Eros frequently shown with bow and arrow, also served as a model for angel representations, as did the Greek messenger god Hermes, son of Zeus.

For a long time, in the Eastern Church it was only possible to distinguish portraits of angels from images of humans by their greater size and their nimbus (or halo). In addition, particularly magnificent garb emphasized the splendor of the angels, who were usually young men. A definitive iconography was later developed by which to represent each angel choir: Seraphim with four fiery-red wings, flaming swords

The earliest representation of a Christian angel is in the Catacomb of Priscilla in Rome. The wall paintings date from the second century.

and bare feet; Cherubim with two blue wings and footwear; Thrones with fiery wheels and four wings spangled with eyes; Dominions, Virtues and Powers with two wings, a long white ecclesiastical tunic, golden belt, and green stole (a sash-like garment that falls from the shoulders), as well as a golden staff terminating in a cross; and, finally, Principalities, Archangels and Malachim (or Angels) with two wings, a spear and a golden belt.

In the Sistine Chapel (shown here in its unrestored state) Michelangelo painted angel-like figures without wings but with sexual characteristics – which the Catholic Church later covered with overpainting.

Armed angels

In the Western Church, representations of angels were quite consistent for hundreds of years, and it was only at the beginning of the thirteenth century that they started to become increasingly differentiated. While demons were equipped with scales and batwings, the nine divine angelic choirs took on the following attributes:

• Seraphim were shown with six wings;
• Cherubim carried an open book;
• Thrones carried a balance;
• Dominions wore royal garb and were equipped with a scepter, imperial orb, and sword;
• Virtues with lilies, red roses, and church garb;
• Powers carried a staff and sword and were armed like knights;
• Principalities wore armor under court dress, and were also equipped with crown, sword, and scepter;
• Archangels were represented as knights in armor or as priests in long, white ecclesiastical tunics;
• Angels, finally, wore church garb and on the forehead a jeweled headband with a cross.

Child angels

From the beginning of the thirteenth century, the Malachim (Angels) were sometimes also shown with plumage. The angels of this choir are associated with a particularly wide array of objects that may appear in depictions of them, including candles, *rotuli* (or scrolls), banners with text, and musical instruments.

In the fourteenth century, images of child angels began to occur, which led to the *putti* (nude boy infants or young children, with or without wings) of the Early Renaissance. Their appearance is reminiscent of the ancient *erotes*, or winged boys, who graced Roman sepulchers.

During the Renaissance, representations of angels became increasingly carnal and masculine. Some of the most famous examples of this epoch come from Michelangelo, the renowned Italian sculptor, painter, architect, and poet (1475–1564). A master of Italy's High and Late Renaissance, Michelangelo created the

The English Romantic William Blake had angelic visions as a child, which affected his artistic work throughout his lifetime.

frescoes in the Vatican's Sistine Chapel. His angel-like figures have no wings, although their genitals were originally shown clearly. The Church, however, had them all removed from sight by painting blue drapery over them; these were removed during a thorough restoration of the chapel in the 1980s–1990s.

An English visionary

The appearance of angels in religious painting changed little from the fifteenth century until a painter was born in the eighteenth century who shared a special connection with angels. Englishman William Blake (1757–1827), a poet, engraver and one of the foremost representatives of English Romanticism, claimed to have learned painting from the angels. As a child he already had angelic visions. By his own account, he saw Jesus—who later dictated many of his texts—almost daily. Blake based his art on his visions and mystical experiences, and claimed to see the souls of deceased people and animals, which he represented in his art.

One of Blake's paintings showing two angels hovering in the tomb over Jesus' body.

Heaven is more than just one vast space. Depending on one's beliefs, it consists of seven to nine separate strata, each inhabited by different groups of angels.

THE SEVEN HEAVENS

It is a little-known fact that there is not just one Heaven, but several. Consider the internationally common idiom *to be in seventh heaven*, which refers to the highest Heaven, the location of the throne of God. This is the highest level of the universe.

The concept of several Heavens is immediately established in the Hebrew word for Heavens, *shamayim*. This is a plural word and it has no singular form; there is no word for an individual Heaven in Hebrew.

Experts are divided over the number of Heavens. Enoch, who claimed to have visited the heavenly realm and described it in the greatest detail, mentioned seven Heavens. Other sources count three Heavens, and others again argue for ten.

The first Heaven: Shamayim/Shamain/Wilon

The first Heaven—called Shamayim, Shamain, or Wilon—borders directly on Earth, and also serves to protect it. At night this Heaven is drawn back (Wilon comes from *velum*, the Latin word for curtain) so that the moon and stars, which occupy a higher Heaven, can be seen. The clouds and wind, however, are located in the first Heaven, as well as two hundred angels who watch over the stars. The patron angels for ice, snow, and the dawn also live there.

The ruler of Shamayim is the Archangel Gabriel. In his narrative about how he arrives at the portal of this Heaven (in the Book of Enoch), Enoch describes it as a vault of ice, clouds, and wind. There was also a river of fire, flowing with flames instead of water.

The Testament of Levi (one of the twelve sons of Jacob and progenitor of the Levite tribe of Israel) also records that the first Heaven contains "fire, snow, and ice made ready for the Day of Judgment, in the righteous judgment of God."

Adam and Eve supposedly lived in the first Heaven—not to be confused with Paradise or the Garden of Eden, which is in the third or fourth Heaven. For Saint Paul, the first Heaven is the Promised Land, in which each tree bears fruit twelve times each year, with different fruits each time. Moreover, this Heaven shines seven times more brightly than silver.

The second Heaven: Raquia/Raqia

The ruler of the second Heaven is also an Archangel, in this case Raphael. The Hebrew word *raqia* means firmament, and in the Talmud it denotes the location of the sun, the moon, and the stars. This Heaven includes the prison of the fallen angels, who wait in chains and complete darkness for the day of the Last Judgment. Enoch and Moses are both supposed to live in another part of this Heaven. According to the Islamic faith, John the Baptist and Jesus Christ also reside in this Heaven. Jesus, who is called Isa bin Miriam, is considered a great prophet—the most important forerunner of Mohammed.

Nine Heavens, or seven?

The ancient Chinese people, as well as the Aztecs, recognized nine Heavens. Ptolemy, the famous Greek mathematician, geographer, and astronomer, identified nine as a cosmic pattern. Hence the Earth lies at the center of the universe, which consists of nine spheres. The poet Dante adopted this scheme for his *Divine Comedy* (see page 39, box).

However, most texts rely on Enoch's account of seven Heavens, and his concept of the Heavens is presented here. Islam also assumes this number: its religious founder, Mohammed, traveled through seven Heavens to come before the throne of God.

Whether these seven Heavens are beside each other, or one above the other, or even represent independent planets outside our solar system (as one bold theory maintains) is a matter of dispute. In the fourteenth century, it was believed that the seven Heavens were connected by means of hooks to seven underlying strata of Earth. These earths, progressing from the seventh to the first, are called Trebbel, Arqa, Nesziah, Tziah, Geh, Adama, and Eres. On the sixth earth, Arqa, is Gehenna, or Hell, with its own seven rings. On this level live strange beings with two heads and holes instead of noses, but also beautiful creatures.

The expression "to be in seventh heaven" is anything but random: seven Heavens are supposed to exist above the human world.

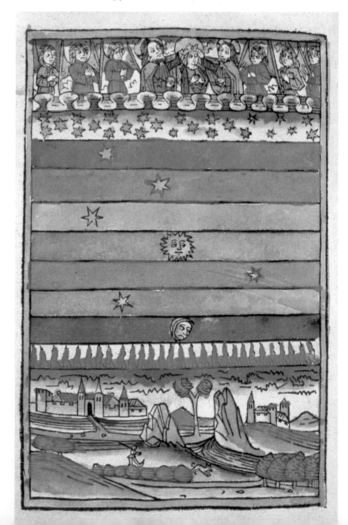

The seven Heavens are the realm not only of the angels, but also their adversaries: thus the fifth Heaven contains a prison for fallen angels, while Lucifer and his demons are held in the third.

The third Heaven: Sagun/Shehaqim

The southern region of the third Heaven is home to the legendary Garden of Eden, also known as Paradise. The word "Eden" derives from the Sumerian *adana*, which translates as "garden." The gateposts of the third Heaven are said to be made of pure gold. Behind them lies an orchard, in which the tree of the life stands, where God Himself rests. Two rivers flow past the Garden of Eden, one brimming with milk and honey, the other one with wine and oil. Three hundred angels guard this idyllic garden. All unblemished souls reach this place after death and receive their reward. Thus there are comforts in this Heaven such as the divine bees, which collect the manna-honey, which is then ground by two massive millstones to the south. These millstones are the source of another name for the third Heaven, *Shehaqim*, which is Hebrew for "millstone."

The ruler of Sagun is the angel Anahel. The Islamic angel of death, Azrael, also lives here. Some sources state that Hell lies in the north of this Heaven, with Lucifer and all his demons.

The fourth Heaven: Zebhul/Machanon

Zebhul, also called Machanon, is described as the location of the heavenly Jerusalem, including the holy temple and the altar of God. In the Apocalypse of Paul he describes the city this way: "it was all of gold, and twelve walls encircled it, and twelve towers inside … And there were twelve gates in the circuit of the city, of great beauty…" Paul described four rivers, one of honey (Phison), one of milk (Euphrates), one of oil (Geon), and one of wine (Tigris).

According to Enoch, Paradise and the Tree of Knowledge are in the fourth Heaven. Whoever eats of its fruit attains wisdom. The great windlass-drawn chariots on which the sun, moon, and the great stars ride is driven to Zebhul. The ruler of this Heaven is the Archangel Michael.

The fifth Heaven: Machon/Methey/Ma'on

In the northern reaches of the fifth Heaven, behind a column blazing with smoke and gargantuan flames, lies a further divine prison. According to some theories, the tenth angel choir (see page 46) is to be found here awaiting its trial. This part of Heaven has neither ground nor sky. In the south of Machon, by contrast, angels sing unceasingly through the night, only falling silent at dawn to let God hear the praises of his people on Earth. The ruler of Machon is either Metatron's brother, Sandalphon, or the angel Sammael. Moses' brother Aaron is said to live in this Heaven, as well as the avenging angels.

The sixth Heaven: Zebul/Makhon

The sixth Heaven is unique in that it is governed by two angels: by Sabbath during the day, and by Zebul at night. Seven Cherubim glorifying God and seven phoenix live here. In Zebul there is an enormous house of knowledge, in which the angels learn everything about humankind, time, and the cosmos. According to Enoch, this Heaven is where angels study in groups and are taught by Archangels. This cold Heaven of freezing temperatures, hail, ice, and snow is also called *Makhon* (Hebrew for "residence"). The prince of the sixth Heaven is the Archangel Gabriel.

The seventh Heaven: Araboth

In the highest realm of Heaven stands the throne of God, around which may be found the angels who are always in his presence: the Cherubim, Seraphim, and Thrones. The prince of Araboth is either the angel Cassiel or the Archangel Michael. The souls of humans not yet born are thought to await their birth in the seventh Heaven.

Paradise is situated in the third Heaven, where it is guarded by 300 angels. Rivers of milk and honey, and of wine and oil flow there.

Adam and Eve being driven out of the Garden of Eden. The prevailing opinion is that they lived in the first Heaven.

ENCOUNTERS WITH ANGELS

The Archangel Michael is said to have appeared several times in this grotto at the pilgrimage center Monte Sant'Angelo in Italy, most recently during the seventeenth century, when he protected the local people from the plague.

FAMOUS SIGHTINGS
OF ANGELS

Reports of angel sightings date not only from Biblical times, but also persist through the ensuing centuries, and even into the twentieth and twenty-first centuries.

Angels don't just appear to people indiscriminately. A person must have lived a very long life in anticipation of a meeting, or lived an especially godly life, to make such a meeting possible. It should not come as a surprise that Catholic popes such as Pius XI (1922–1939) and John XXIII (1958–1963) spoke of being in close contact with their guardian angels.

Curing the plague

In the early Middle Ages, the Archangel Michael is said to have appeared in Apulia, a region in southeastern Italy. Today's pilgrimage center of Monte Sant'Angelo is located at the site of his repeated appearances. Michael's first appearance was to the holy bishop of Sipontum, named Laurentius, to whom he explained that this mountain grotto was his holy place and protected by him. Every petition made inside this grotto would be granted. Later, the Archangel himself consecrated the grotto, and even today it remains the only Christian shrine that has not been sanctified by the Church. The Archangel appeared in the grotto for the last time in the year 1656, when the plague had broken out at Monte Gargano and the archbishop therefore summoned him. Michael appeared and taught people to use the grotto's stones to heal the disease. It is believed that the plague was overcome in the region this way.

In the year 708, the Archangel Michael is said to have appeared on the rocky French islet of Mont-Saint-Michel—which still bears his name—and to have demanded that a church be built there. Both the island and the church are very popular pilgrim and tourist destinations.

Saint Pio of Pietralcina (1887–1968), like Francis of Assisi, is known to have borne the stigmata (see page 27, box). It is not known, however, with which angels he came into contact. Padre Pio was embarrassed by the wounds in his hands and feet, and wore fingerless gloves to cover the marks. Born the son of a poor farmer in a small village near Naples, Padre Pio had planned to become a modest priest-farmer. But things turned out differently: he became famous as a prophet and faith healer. He is said to have predicted the elevation of young Karol Wojtyla (later Pope John Paul II, 1978–2005) to the head of the Catholic Church, and later the assassination attempt made on him in 1981, as well. Saint Pio is also credited with the rare gift of bilocation (see page 28, box), which is the ability to be in two places at once.

A spear in the soul

Padre Pio described the angel that appeared to him as a bright figure, a majestic man, "of rare beauty and radiating like the sun." From that point forward, the angel supported him in his fight against evil. This angel also prophesied to him that God's final victory was assured. In 1918, as Padre Pio was hearing the confession of some young people, he received his first sacred wounds from an angel holding a long iron blade in his hand, with fire spurting from its extremely sharp point. The angel thrust the point into Padre Pio, into his very soul, causing him great pain.

In the autumn of the same year, an angel appeared to him bleeding profusely at the hands, feet, and chest. Padre Pio described this meeting: "The sight appalled me. I cannot describe to you how I felt at that moment. I felt like I was dying and certainly would have died if the Lord had not intervened and held my heart, which threatened to leap from my chest." He continued, "the apparition faded, and I noticed that my hands, feet, and side were pierced and blood was pouring from them. Try to imagine the agonies I experienced at that time and still suffer nearly every day!"

Padre Pio received insights into the deepest secrets of those in the confessional as he heard their confessions, shown to him by their guardian angels. Angels are also believed to have given him the power to understand foreign languages. In the year 2002, Padre Pio was canonized as Saint Pio of Pietralcina by Pope John Paul II.

Unlike these examples, however, most documented angel apparitions take place in the presence of women.

Padre Pio, who was canonized as Saint Pio in 2002, is said to have spoken with many guardian angels.

The perfect bride of Christ

Blessed Angela of Foligno (1248–1309) is recognized as "a perfect bride of Christ." After she had repented of her earlier sins and devoted herself to God, the Savior and his angels appeared to her in numerous vivid visions. As Blessed Angela wrote, "If I had not experienced it myself, I would not believed possible the indescribable blessedness the sight of an angel can bestow."

The saint and founding abbess Agnes of Montepulciano (1247–1317) received communion at the hands of an angel ten times. Angels appeared several times to Saint Risa of Viterbo (1235–1252) and, among

The French national heroine and saint Joan of Arc was told by the Archangel Michael that she had been chosen to save her country.

other things, predicted future events such as the death of Emperor Frederick II.

Saint Clare of Montefalco, also known as Saint Clare of the Cross (ca. 1275–1308), was a beautiful girl from a wealthy family who had already devoted herself to God at the age of six. She led a penitent and Spartan life, always going barefoot and sleeping on hard boards, and eating nothing but bitter herbs and brown bread. Angels appeared to her as winged boys. When Saint Clare's heart was examined after her death, it was found to contain an image of the crucified Christ.

Angels appeared to her sister, Joan of Montefalco, as well, accompanied by heavenly music. The other women of her religious community could hear these sounds, and also described how Joan's room was flooded with light during the apparitions.

Rescue by an angel

Saint Francesca of Rome (1384–1440)—also known as Francesca Romana, and "Ceccolella" or "Ciccolella" ("Little Frances")—and her sister-in-law Vannuza were saved from drowning in the Tiber River by an angel in 1399. It looked like a long-haired boy of about ten years old wearing a white ecclesiastical raiment. The angel remained with her for another twenty-five years, helping in her struggle against the Devil, who tormented her in the form of demonic visions.

Later, a more radiant angel took his place, and the second one remained near her until she died. By the light of this angel, who always stood at her side, she could read and write in the darkest night. Saint Francesca often saw this second angel weaving with a golden thread of spider's silk, which she recognized to be the thread of her own life. According to legend, she saw shortly before her death that the fabric was almost complete.

The maid of Orléans

The patron saint of France, Joan of Arc (1412–1431)—also known as Joan of Orléans—received a vision of the Archangel Michael at the age of thirteen, in which he announced that she had been chosen to save France from England, which occupied part of the country at

In Montepulciano in Tuscany, Saint Agnes received communion from angels several times. She later founded an abbey there.

that time, and help the rightful king, Charles VII, be crowned at Reims. Michael appeared to her as a radiant young knight, surrounded by other angels, but he did not stay long at this first meeting. Later, however, Michael became a kind of divine companion for Joan.

The angel stood by her, supporting her at critical moments. He helped her find a lost sword and continually reminded her of her purpose. When the Inquisition interrogated Joan of Arc after her capture, she told them that feet of the Archangel Michael had imprinted the ground. This was regarded as a heretical statement, and Joan of Arc was burned at the stake in Rouen.

Sweat and blood

Saint Gemma Galgani (1879–1903) lived a short life full of suffering. As a young girl she lost her mother, her brother, and finally also her father. Her health was poor and she received extreme unction at twenty-one. Afterwards, however, she experienced a miraculous recovery and worked as a housemaid. Some time later, on the evening before the Catholic Feast of the Sacred Heart (which is no longer well-known), she fell into an ecstasy and the stigmata appeared on her body, which flowed with sweat and blood. This was repeated with great pain every Thursday until her death on Easter Saturday, 1903. "Christ lives in me," she said about it. Gemma was on familiar terms with her guardian angel, which she saw near her almost all the time, and which treated her in an almost maternal way, praising or scolding her. She could also see other peoples' angels.

The stigmata
The stigmata are the manifestation of the sacred wounds of Christ on the hands, feet, chest, and head (caused by the crown of thorns), which he received at the crucifixion. Most people with stigmata belong to the Roman Catholic church, but there are similar people in the Anglican, Evangelical, and Methodist churches, as well as in other Christian sects. Several hundred cases of stigmatization have been claimed so far (almost exclusively women), but only thirteen are officially recognized by the Catholic church.

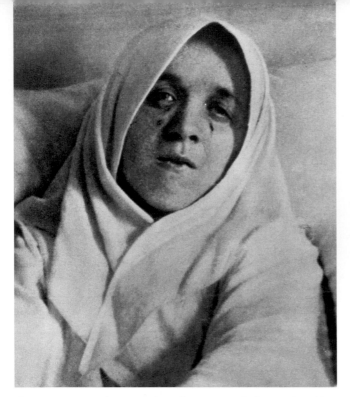
Therese Neumann of Germany bore the stigmata of Christ and could speak with guardian angels.

Meetings with an Archangel

Further contemporary meetings with angels are known in addition to the life of Padre Pio. The German mystic Therese Neumann lived from 1898 to 1962 and became famous as Resl of Konnersreuth. Like Padre Pio, she came from a simple farming family. After a serious illness, she began to have visions every Friday. Stigmata appeared on her beginning in 1926, and for thirty-six years afterwards, she ate nothing other than Communion wafers, which she received with the Eucharist. Therese Neumann is also said to have had the gift of bilocation.

She described her guardian angel as a wingless "being of light." By her own account, it continually protected her from the Devil. Therese Neumann is also believed to have seen the guardian angels of her various visitors, and to have observed some of the angels carrying out their assignments—including, for example, the Archangel Gabriel informing Mary that she would give birth a son, Jesus. During her visions, she reportedly spoke in languages that no simple peasant girl could possibly have known, such as Hebrew and Aramaic. Today, however, the Catholic Church does not officially recognize either her stigmatization or her sustenance from Communion wafers alone.

An angel like a butterfly

The Italian mystic Teresa Palminota (1896–1934) enjoyed a particularly affectionate bond with her guardian angel. She called him her "Dear Angel," and it reportedly encouraged her through all the vicissitudes of life. It is even claimed that "Dear Angel" typed a letter for her when Teresa was not able to do so. When Teresa left her home, Dear Angel accompanied her in the form of a white butterfly, which fluttered all around her. According to reports, this guardian angel helped Teresa Palminota overcome her handicap in the confessional. As a result of a severe ear infection, she had become completely deaf. Yet she apparently understood her father confessor in spite of this, even though she could not see him to read his lips. Teresa Palminota said that God or her Dear Angel let her understand everything.

There are contemporary examples of women in direct contact with their angels, too. Natuzza Evolo is a stigmatic visionary and faith healer who lives in Calabria, Italy. This mother and grandmother of many reports having the gift of being able to see nearly everyone's guardian angels close beside them. However, these angels are to be found only with living people, as the dead no longer have divine companions. The angels always stand to the right of ordinary people, but they stand to the left of clergy, making it possible for her to recognize them even when they aren't in ecclesiastical dress.

Bilocation
This term derives from the Latin (bi-locus, two places), and denotes just that: a person's simultaneous presence in two separate places. Saints and mystics, as well as yogis and shamans, are all accredited with this ability. The Catholic Church explains the phenomenon with the fact that such a person's desire to do good is so strong that they can fulfill their obligations in two places at once. Well-known examples include the Dominican monk Martin de Porres, Saint Pio, and Saint Anthony of Padua, as well as the Swedish mystic Emanuel Swedenborg (see page 74 ff).

Divine images of blood

Natuzza Evolo is also reported to have manifested hemography—images on her body drawn in blood that form religious words or symbols. These have also been found on handkerchiefs and other articles of clothing that came into contact with Natuzza Evolo's stigmata. This occurred for the first time when she was sixteen years old and was confirmed in the church in Mileto. At that time she had not yet experienced the stigmata, but a bloody cross formed on her shoulder. A paranormal observation study (research into instances of extrasensory perception and psychokinesis that are not explainable by scientific means) did not result in any evidence that Natuzza Evolo was a charlatan. She takes no payment for services she renders for people—she donates it to others—and tries to stem the public interest in her.

Teresa Palminota was always accompanied by her guardian angel. When other people were around, it appeared as a white butterfly.

Angels appear as helpers to people in distress, or as divine messengers, as the angel of the Annunciation, pictured here.

After six angel visitations and six visions of the Virgin, the Portuguese village of Fátima became one of the most important Catholic pilgrim destinations in the world.

THE ANGELS OF FÁTIMA

The most famous visions of the Virgin Mary in the twentieth century took place in the Portuguese village of Fátima. Far fewer people know that six angel visitations preceded the six visions of the Virgin, which were intended as preparation for the Second Coming.

The first three angel sightings, seen by the eight-year-old Lucia dos Santos and two other young girls, took place in 1915. Lucia later described a snow white form that hovered above the trees, silently, then quickly vanished. This was repeated twice more. In retrospect, this was interpreted as an attempt to familiarize the children gently with this extrasensory phenomenon so they could become receptive to it.

The angel of peace

More of these floating and vanishing forms followed in 1916. An angel addressed three Catholic shepherd children: Lucia (now ten years old), her cousin Francisco Marto (nine years old), and his sister Jacinta. During a rainstorm, the three children had sought shelter from the storm in a cave. When they peered out of the cave following a strong gust of wind, they saw a white shape above the trees in front of the cave, moving toward them. It was a gloriously beautiful boy of about fifteen years old. Lucia later described this meeting precisely: "As he came closer and closer to us, he said, 'Don't be afraid! I am the Angel of Peace. Pray with me.' Then he knelt down and touched the soil with his forehead. Moved by a supernatural power, we did as he did and repeated the words we heard him saying."

Some three months later, when the three children were playing in the vegetable garden, the angel returned and this time requested them to pray unceasingly and to make sacrifices on behalf of all people. The children did as they were told and some months later, while they were praying in the cave as the angel had shown them, the angel reappeared—even more radiant this time than it had been before.

In his hand he held a chalice, on which lay a communion wafer with blood dripping from it. The angel knelt as the radiantly lit cup and communion wafer floated upwards. After the angel and the children said a prayer together, the angel handed Lucia the communion wafer and let the other two children drink from the chalice. With this, they were ready to encounter the Virgin Mary, who entrusted three secrets to them. Between May and October 1917, in each case on the 13th of the month, she appeared to them in open countryside. As a result, Fátima became an important Catholic pilgrimage center, which, like Lourdes in France, is visited by the sick in the hope they will be healed. At her last appearance, ten thousand onlookers are reported to have been present and to have witnessed the same miracle involving the sun. All of them could look at the sun—which resembled a silver disc and revolved like a wheel of fire—without pain. Even the New York Times reported on the event.

Lucia dos Santos, 93, was one of the three peasant children to whom the Virgin and the angel appeared.

The angel that appeared to the shepherd children charged them to pray in a cave. Little Jacinta Marto was one of the three children.

The May 1981 attempted assassination of Pope John Paul II in St. Peter's Square, Rome, had been predicted by the shepherd children of Fátima.

The vision of the attempted assassination of the pope

The secrets that Mary revealed to the children in those encounters included terrible visions of Hell, World War II, the danger of communist Russia, and the assassination attempt on Pope John Paul II (who was badly wounded by a gunshot in 1981). The mysteries also touched upon the significance of the cult of the Virgin.

As part of the third revelation, which Lucia set down in writing, an important task is ascribed to an angel. "After the two parts I have already described, we saw an angel holding a fiery sword in its left hand, slightly above and to the left of Our Dear Lady; the angel sprayed sparks, and flames went forth from it, as if to set the whole world on fire; but the flames were extinguished when they came into contact with the light streaming from the right hand of Our Dear Lady. Then the angel, pointing to the Earth with his right hand, called out in a loud voice, 'Repent! Repent! Repent!'"

Our Dear Lady is a reference to the Virgin Mary.

In the next passage, Lucia described an assassination attempt on the pope, as well as the shooting of other ecclesiastics and lay victims by soldiers. All of these events took place on a hill that was crowned with a cross. In her report she adds, "under the two arms of the cross were two angels, each one with a crystal watering can in its hand. In these, they gathered the blood of the martyrs, and with it they soaked the souls approaching God."

From their first appearance to the final vision of Mary, then, the angels of Fátima played both of their two important roles—both as divine messengers and servants of Heaven.

The psychoanalyst C.G. Jung thought of angels as energy complexes.

Visions of the Virgin

The Roman Catholic Church has also officially endorsed other visions of the Virgin in addition to Fátima. In Europe, the French village of Lourdes is the most famed. In 1858, the Virgin Mary appeared there several times to the young Bernadette Soubirous (1844–1879). The grotto of Massabielle, where Bernadette opened a spring during a vision, is highly regarded as a place of healing today.

The greatest Marian pilgrimage center in the world, however, is in Mexico. In Guadaloupe, in the year 1531, a brown-skinned girl appeared to the recently baptized Juan Diego, alone. She identified herself as the Virgin Mary and insisted that he establish a shrine for her there. The bishop did not believe Juan Diegos, whereupon Maria caused roses to grow at the site of the visitation. Juan Diego wove these into a cloak and brought it to the bishop. The portrait of this dark-skinned Mary appeared on the cloak.

Other officially recognized visions of the Virgin took place in the village of Banneaux in the Ardennes and in the French hamlet of La Salette. Visions of Mary that have been occurring on the 25th of each month at Medugorje (a tiny spot in Bosnia-Herzegovina) since June 24,1981, have not yet been confirmed by the Church.

The Virgin Mary appeared to Saint Bernadette of Lourdes quite often.

POSSIBLE EXPLANATIONS

Within the field of psychology, angel apparitions are usually treated as hallucinations or delusions, in accordance with the principle that people see what they expect to see.

The Swiss psychoanalyst Carl Gustav Jung (1875–1961), on the other hand, suggested an alternative scientific explanation for the phenomenon of angel apparitions. In his analytical work, Jung always probed those bizarre elements of his patients' dreams that could not be explained by their personal histories. Many of these elements appeared in myths, fairy tales or legends, however, and they always triggered strong feelings in his patients.

C.G. Jung called these 'archetypes' and later defined them as energy complexes, which only emerge in modern times through dreams, neuroses, or delusions.

Angels as energy complexes

According to Jung, contemporary humans have lost the ability to connect consciously with these archetypes—which, along with the (acquired) individual unconscious and the (shared) collective unconscious, determine the human psyche.

Jung argues that archetypes have the function of bringing the human personality as a whole into alignment. These energy complexes cause the appearance of archetypal images in the human conscious on their behalf. Thus, divine apparitions can occur that bring the soul back into balance. In this way, they fulfill the same role that is attributed to angels, helping people in distress.

THE HIERARCHY OF ANGELS

The three Archangels Michael, Raphael (here with Tobit), and Gabriel are the only three angels mentioned by name in the Bible.

ANGELS IN CHRISTIANITY

Concepts of the nature of angels differ substantially from one religion or religious community to another. Even within a single religion, there are varying schools of thought and opinion on how to evaluate the role of angels in the universe.

For this reason, the official views of the Roman Catholic Church are presented first. With over a billion faithful worldwide, Roman Catholicism is the largest denomination within Christianity (which, with two billion faithful, is the world's dominant religion).

The word angel is derived from the Greek word *àngelos* (messenger). This, in turn, is a translation of the Hebrew term *mal'ach*, which has the same meaning.

One of the religious controversies within Catholicism concerns the existence of incorporeal spiritual entities called angels. According to Saint Augustine,

the designation "angel" describes the function, but not the nature, of the beings: "If you ask about its nature, then it is a spirit; if you ask about its office, then it is an angel: according to its nature, it is a spirit; according to its behavior, an angel." (Psalm 103; 1, 15).

Purely spiritual beings

Angels are the servants and messengers of God. Thus they "... always behold the face of my Father who is in Heaven," (Matthew 18:10) and are obedient "... mighty ones who do his word, hearkening to the voice of his word!" (Psalm 103:20)

Angels are considered purely spiritual but individual entities that possess understanding and free will. Pope

John Paul II (1978–2005) said, "The angels have no 'body' (even if, in particular circumstances, they reveal themselves under visible forms because of their mission for the good of men[sic])." They tower above all visible creatures in perfection, and they have existed since the world began.

The center of the angel world is Christ, who is above the angels, as the following passage from the Bible affirms: "And again, when he brings the firstborn into the world, he says, 'Let all God's angels worship him'." (Hebrews 1:6)

As purely spiritual entities, angels are also immortal, which may be inferred from another passage, found in the Book of Luke: "for they cannot die any more, because they are equal to angels and children of God, being children of the resurrection." (Luke 20:36)

Angels accompany human beings from birth to death and intercede on our behalf. Saint Basil, bishop of Caesarea, wrote: "An angel accompanies every one of the faithful as a protector and shepherd, in order to lead him to the life." (Basilius, Contra Eunonium 3,1)

The Catholic Church especially honors three angels, who are the only ones specifically named in the Bible. These are the Archangels Michael (see page 49), Gabriel (see page 50) and Raphael (see page 51).

Pope John Paul II also believed in angels. He viewed them as spiritual entities who could also take physical form.

Unforgivable sin

If an angel sins, God considers this a far more serious offense than when humans sin. God will never forgive an angel, since these heavenly beings were created good by Him, but fell from grace and became evil by their own free will. In the Letter of Jude (verse 6) we read: "And the angels that did not keep their own position but left their proper dwelling have been kept by him in eternal chains in the nether gloom until the judgment of the great day." When angels reject divine truth, this is unforgivable in light of their spiritual perfection and sharp intellect, which is obviously superior to humans'.

It says in the First Book of John that "... the whole world is in the power of the evil one." (1 John 5:19) The Devil tried without success to tempt Jesus to worship him instead of God. The Devil has had more success in this with certain people, of whom it is said that they are "possessed by the Devil." According to Jesus, "this kind cannot be driven out by anything but prayer." (Mark 9:29)

Saint Augustine—church father, philosopher, and bishop of Hippo—concerned himself with the existence of angels early on.

THE ANGEL TRIADS OF DIONYSIUS THE AREOPAGITE

Christianity recognizes nine angelic choirs, organized into three triads.

According to the Acts of the Apostles (17:34), Dionysius was a member of the highest city council in Athens, the Court of Areopagus, and was therefore given the surname Aeropagita. Converted by Saint Paul on Mount Areopagus, he became the first bishop of Athens. His name appears as the author of texts dating from the fifth or sixth century. In these he describes his conversion by the apostle Paul and how he saw the solar eclipse that accompanied Christ's death, in the Egyptian city of Heliopolis. These texts also relate that he was present with the apostles at the burial of Jesus' mother, Mary. Until the nineteenth century, it was accepted that Dionysius the Areopagite was indeed the author of these important works. Today, however, scholarly consensus is that the texts were not written by Dionysius himself, but by an unknown author of the Late Antique period, probably a Syrian monk.

The works of Dionysius the Areopagite:

De caelesti hierarchia
(The Celestial Hierarchy)

De ecclesiastica hierarchia
(The Ecclesiastical Hierarchy)

De mystica Theologia
(The Mystical Hierarchy)

De divinis nominibus
(The Divine Names)

The work of Dionysius the Areopagite represented the first great systematization of teaching about angels. Originally the name for a divine messenger alone, Dionysius used the term 'angel' to embrace all spiritual entities who serve the kingdom of Heaven.

According to Dionysius, the hierarchy comprises three sets of three choirs. In the enlightened upper triad, in descending order, are the Seraphim, Cherubim, and Thrones. In the middle triad, in descending order, are the Dominions, Virtues, and Powers. Finally, in the lower triad, in descending order, we find the Principalities, Archangels, and simple Angels (or Malachim).

Later theologians, such as Thomas Aquinas (see box), based their writings on this angel scholarship. But there were other models that mapped out a different organization. According to Pope Gregory the Great (590–604), Seraphim and Cherubim alone form the highest class, beholding and glorifying God as they encircle Him. The second group consists of five choirs that do God's work in the cosmos and in the world. The third group in this scheme is responsible for people. However, unlike Dionysius the Areopagite's organization, it consists of only two choirs, Archangels and Angels.

Nonetheless, Dionysius' *Celestial Hierarchy* remains the most famous and important work on angels in Christianity. According to Dionysius, the angels are immaculate, comparable with perfect mirrors that reflect the rays of heavenly light and shine with a holy radiance so that others can follow them.

Dionysius, as well as the later Saint Thomas Aquinas, divided the angels into three hierarchies of three choirs each. These circle the holy throne of God, something like the planets of our solar system in their orbits around the sun. This concept strongly informed ideas about the organization of the kingdom of Heaven.

According to Dionysius, God works through his messengers, the angels, who announce or implement his will to humans. God is a stream of power, which consists of and radiates pure ideas. The further these ideas get from God, the weaker their vibrations become. They transform into light and become the first sphere around the heavenly throne. Farther away from God this light becomes matter. The vibrations of the angels thus become gradually weaker from the first choir to the last.

Thomas Aquinas

The Italian nobleman Thomas Aquinas (1225–1274) studied in both Paris and Cologne, and is considered the greatest Catholic theologian of all time. He left an extensive collection of writings and was canonized as a saint in 1323.

In his *Summa Theologica*, he set up a heavenly status system, dividing the angels into three hierarchies of three choirs each. The first hierarchy—Seraphim, Cherubim, Thrones—was assigned to the service of God's throne. Seraphim symbolize the highest reflection of God's love, and pray continuously to God; Cherubim represent the reflection of divine wisdom; Thrones stand for illumination of the divine majesty. The choirs of the second hierarchy—Dominions, Powers, and Princes—are compared to medieval princes, who administer the a king's estates. The angels of the third hierarchy—Virtues, Archangels, Malachim (angels)—are responsible for tending to humanity.

The apostle Paul converted Dionysius, who later became one of the most important angel theorists.

The Divine Comedy

The Italian poet Dante Alighieri (1256–1321) also drew on the work of Dionysius the Areopagite in his *Divine Comedy*. This epic poem, written in the first person, consists of three cantos: *Inferno* (Hell), *Purgatorio* (Purgatory), and *Paradiso* (Paradise). Despite its title, the poem is not a comedy, but the description of a journey to God, in which Dante also tells of nine spheres whirling around a common center. This pivotal work of world literature introduced Dionysius' angel hierarchy to a much wider audience and solidified its importance even into modern times.

Probably the most famous Cherubim in art were painted by Raphael.

THE UPPER TRIAD:
IN GOD'S IMMEDIATE PRESENCE

The angels of the upper triad are incorporeal light forms. They can also manifest themselves in material form. Although they are close to the strong light radiated by God as the center of the cosmos, these heavenly beings are not injured by it, while all others are burned by its intensity. The only exception is some of the Archangels. Archangels belong simultaneously to the eighth choir but also to higher ones, and in part even stand above these; they therefore share characteristics of the higher angels.

Triad

The term *trias* stands for a group of three in both Latin and Greek. In Ancient Egypt, the three symbols of power were known as the triad. In religion, a three-fold god is understood as a triad. Jupiter, Juno, and Minerva formed one such in Ancient Rome; and in Hinduism there are the gods Brahma, Vishnu, and Shiva. In contrast, the Christian Trinity is not a triad, but a tri-unity, because the three entities—Father, Son, and Holy Ghost—are viewed as a single whole.

The first choir: Seraphim

Seraphim—the angelic choir that stands nearest to God—are beings of pure light and pure thought. But they can also appear to humans in physical form. According to descriptions, on those occasions they have six wings: with two wings they cover their face, with two they cover their feet, and with two they fly (Isaiah 6:2). Isaiah also described the Seraphim as "the burning ones" that burned away sin with their flames. In addition, they can inflame the true, divine love within people.

The name Seraphim probably comes from the Hebrew words *hebra* (perfect one) and *ser* (higher spirit). However, some researchers see a connection with the Persian term *serapis* or *saraphen,* for animal forms with snake heads.

According to Enoch, there are only four Seraphim, and he assigns them to the four winds or the four points of the compass. In contrast to this, later theologians assumed the existence of four spirits that are even above the Seraphim, ruled by the Archangel Metatron (also equated with Michael). Others regard Metatron as the most powerful Seraph. Satan may also be a Seraph.

In paintings, Seraphim frequently carry fiery swords and flaming torches.

The second choir: Cherubim

The Cherubim were immortalized on the Ark of the Covenant. This chest was one of the most holy objects in the Bible. In the New Testament (Hebrews 9:4), it is described as a gilded acacia wood chest containing "a golden urn of manna and Aaron's rod that budded" (Aaron was high priest in Moses' time), as well as the Tablets of the Law (two stone tablets inscribed with the Ten Commandments that were given to Moses by God on Mount Sinai). On the lid of the Ark of the Covenant were two Cherubim spreading their wings protectively over the chest.

In the Garden of Eden this angelic choir functions as a guard. Here, God set the Cherubim with a fiery sword to guard the entrance to the Tree of Life, as it is called in the Book of Genesis.

Cherubim have four wings and four faces. The prophet Ezekiel describes this more precisely: a man's face to the front, a lion's face to the right, a bull's face to the left, and an eagle's face to the rear. When the Cherubim move, the noise of their wings is like the sound of a great deluge, like the voice of the Almighty. Cherubim have feet in the shape of bull's hooves that shine like bright, burnished copper.

Cherubim are both the bearers of God's throne as well as its charioteers.

The Hebrew word *kerub* means "one who intercedes" (derived from the Assyrian word *karibu*), and can also be translated as "abundance of divine knowledge." The best-known Cherubim are the Archangels Gabriel and Uriel.

The third choir: Thrones

This group of angels (also called Thronoi, Ophanim, or Galgallin) is the most mysterious of all the choirs. In various sources the Thrones are referred to as "great wheels" when they materialize on Earth. Their Hebrew names also underline this classification, since *ofan* and *galgal* mean wheel. The Thrones most often appear with the Cherubim in their role as charioteers. The prophet Ezekiel provided a detailed description of the chariot of God, in which the Cherubim steer and the Thrones act as wheels. The "fiery ember" is also understood as a description of the Thrones.

As the lowest choir of the upper triad, the Thrones stand adjacent to the middle triad, and thus to the material Heaven. They therefore have the task of using their wings as a shield to protect the lower angels from the searing vibrations of the Cherubim and Seraphim. The Archangel Raphael is understood to be the regent of this sphere.

The mysterious angelic choir: the Thrones, which are also often manifested as great wheels.

Camael in the role of a good angel, comforting Jesus in the Garden of Gethsemane before Judas betrays him. But a dark side is also attributed to Camael.

THE MIDDLE TRIAD: DIVINE EQUILIBRIUM

The second triad of angels has an intermediary function. The most important task of the Dominions, Virtues, and Powers is to achieve oneness with God: they attempt to resolve such opposites as matter and spirit, good and evil.

In the Middle Ages, the angels of the middle triad were frequently embodied in simple garb, usually white, floor-length albs or tunics. This raiment was generally fastened with a golden belt, and they wore a green stole over their shoulders. A gold staff was usually held in their right hand and the seal of God in their left.

The fourth choir: Dominions

The first choir of the middle triad fulfills this intermediary function most clearly. The Dominions (also called *kyriotetes* [Greek: lordship, authority], hashmallin, or hamshallim) are well-known as intermediaries of divine grace. They act from the center of the cosmos—God—toward the lower spheres. Their name originates from the Hebrew *himshil*, meaning "appointed rulers." But they have another task within the realm of angels, as well, which is to oversee the divine hierarchy and maintain proper order.

In addition, "the divine letters of the holy name" (a circumlocution for the true name of God) are thought to be preserved in their sphere.

The angels Zadkiel (grace of God), Yahriel, and Muriel (divine Gift) are named as the highest of the Dominions. The best-known angel of the Dominions, however, is Hasmal (also Hashmal or Chasmal), "the fire-speaking angel." As an indication of their authority, these four are often shown in pictures holding a scepter or imperial orb in one hand.

The fifth choir: Virtues

With respect to its duties, the fifth choir has strong similarities with the guardian angels. The Virtues (also called Malakim, Dynameis or Tarshishim) achieve divine miracles. They are the ones who fight for good alongside the beleaguered faithful. They help humans in times of need, giving them courage and strength, which is why they are characterized as angels of mercy.

Two of the names for this choir are derived from the Hebrew: *mal'ach* means "angels," and *Tarshish* is a Biblical expression for a distant, mythical country. Their most famous appearance in the Bible occurred at the ascension of Christ: Jesus was borne into Heaven by two Virtues.

The Virtues are led by the Archangels Michael, Gabriel, and Raphael as well as the angels Tarshish, Bariel and—prior to his forcible expulsion from Heaven by Michael—Satanel.

The sixth choir: Powers

The Powers (also called Dynamis and Potentiates, or authorities) are believed to be the first angelic choir that God created. They reside in a region of transition, in this case between the second and third triad, and act as powerful border guards there.

Powers are the armed forces of Heaven in the fight against the Devil and his demons.

An ambiguous angel

The high prince of the Powers, the sixth angelic choir, is Camael. According Simon Magus, who lived in the first century, Camael is one of seven angels who stand in the very presence of God, and he commands 144,000 militant angels. Sources conflict about whether Camael is good or evil. In Jewish lore, he is said to have tried to prevent Moses receiving the Torah from God. On the other hand, Camael had the important duty of appearing to Jesus as he prayed in the Garden of Gethsemane the night before his crucifixion, just before Judas Iscariot betrayed him.

Camael is also occasionally described as a Prince of Hell in leopard form. In the occult, he is known as a ruler of the war planet Mars.

Dionysius the Areopagite wrote that it is thanks to the Powers, Heaven's steadfast army, constantly battling against Hell, that the forces of evil did not overtake the world a long time ago. But their proximity to the demons—and thus to temptation—is also dangerous for the Powers; thus it is not surprising that most of the fallen angels come from their ranks.

The angel Beleth, for example, was once a great prince of this choir. He now commands eighty-five demonic legions in Hell. The former angel Carniveau, now a demon, is associated with many witches' sabbaths. The angel Uvall (Vual, Voval, Uval) became a kind of devil-panderer in the form of a camel, who procures women for his 'clientele.' Like the highest prince of the Powers, Camael (he who sees God; see box), it is not clearly established whether Uvall is good or evil.

In addition to their role as border guards, the Powers are also responsible for humans' souls. Their goal is to balance the opposing forces of good and evil that surround us; thus they are also described as spiritual guides or leaders.

THE LOWER TRIAD: THE HANDS OF GOD

The lower triad is the closest to the human realm, which is why these angels are more susceptible than all the others to potential dangers, attacks, and injuries. Similarly, none are so close to temptations, especially those of the carnal kind, which can also lead angels into temptation and away from their intended path. And indeed, this has cost many angels their place in Heaven.

In the art of the Middle Ages, the representation of this triad developed its own symbolic language. Military dress such as an army uniform or armor, along with weapons such as the lance or battle-axe, are indications of angels of the lower triad. Over time, however, their martial appearance gave way to simple garments with ribbons, while their weapons were exchanged for the Christian symbol for purity and innocence, the white Madonna lily.

The seventh choir: Principalities

Humans and their cities lie under the protection of the Principalities (also called Princes or Archai). Today religion is also listed among its spheres of responsibility, as well as the entire material universe.

Nisroch is named by many sources as head of the Principalities. This angel was once a mortal human who was elevated to the Assyrian godhead, whence he received the head of an eagle. Occultists, however, reject his role as an angel of the Principalities and see him as a commander in chief of the demonic army.

Another angel who is always named in connection with the leadership of the Principalities is Anael (also Barakiel). He is considered one of the seven angels of creation. Anael is ruler of the second Heaven and responsible for all prayers that ascend from the first Heaven. He is also in charge of all earthly rulers, as well as the terrestrial moon. Many sources also see Anael as the angel in the celestial hierarchy responsible for sexuality and fertility.

After these, Hamiel and Cervill are the best-known angels of the Principalities. The angel Hamiel may have been the one that bore the patriarch Enoch (from the Hebrew *hanoks*, the initiate) into Heaven. Hamiel is equally well-known by the name of Ishtar, a Sumerian queen of Heaven. Cervill is known as the Prince of strength, and it was he who helped David to defeat the giant Goliath with a stone catapult.

Angels of the lower triad can often be recognized by a white Madonna lily, which stands for purity and innocence.

The eighth choir: Archangels

The lower triad includes what are probably the most famous angels of all, the Archangels, also well-known as the "heavenly hosts." The prefix "arch" is derived from the Greek *arche*, meaning first or highest. The Archangels are first in two complementary respects. After the guardian angels, they are the first angels in proximity to humans. At the same time they are also the first angels with God—not in terms of their spatial proximity to the divine light, but in terms of their meaning. In the Book of Revelation, the Archangels are the ones who stand in the presence of God; and they are often entrusted with the traditional role of messenger, communicating divine revelations to humans. In addition, they are the commanders of the divine legions in the fight against the hoards of Hell.

There is considerable discrepancy about Archangels in the sources, such as their number and who is ranked among them (see page 48).

The ninth choir: Malachim

The ninth angel choir can unequivocally be characterized as the divine infantry (foot soldiers). They are often simply called angels, and are also known as Angelos, Throng, Vision (Daniel 10:7), Spirit (Revelation 1:4), Malak, Malakh or *Malach*. The latter name originates from the Hebrew, where it means simply "messenger." In the ancient Indian language of Sanskrit, the term *angeres* means a divine spirit, and in Persian, the usual word is *angaros*, which can also be translated as "message-bearing."

The exact number of Malachim thought to exist differs widely from source to source. The Hebrew patriarch Enoch went with a precise 301,655,722. In the thirteenth century, however, the bishop of Tusculum, in contrast, cited almost 400,000,000 angels (see also page 60).

Ancient Hebrew sources suggest that new Malachim are created with God's every breath. Unlike the higher choirs, however, these angels are not thought to be entities of pure light and spirit, but material beings. Nonetheless, the Catholic church today regards all angels as immaterial spirits.

Guardian angels come to the aid of people in distress, either through deeds or counsel.

Guardian angels

It is not clear whether guardian angels are a subgroup of the Malachim, or whether all angels of this choir should be called guardian angels. The most famed Archangels—Michael, Raphael, Gabriel, and Uriel—are also counted among the guardian angels, and are even their leaders. According to the oldest sources, there are seventy guardian angels, whose leader is Michael. Over time, however, this has expanded to hundreds of thousands.

According to a passage in Matthew (18:10), everyone has a guardian angel: "See that you do not despise one of these little ones; for I tell you that in Heaven their angels always behold the face of my Father who is in Heaven."

Because of their indiscretions, the Grigori were destroyed by God in the Flood.

The tenth choir: Grigori

The tenth choir, the Grigori, is an anomaly: according to prevailing theological opinion, this tenth angel choir no longer exists, because God destroyed it in the Great Flood. Until the thirteenth century, this choir was not even acknowledged.

Carnal desire

But the Church had a problem, because the Bible says that angels pleasured themselves with human women for whom they felt physical desire—despite the fact that they were officially sexless! Thus an angelic choir was created—and it was the bishop of Paris who announced the existence of this unusual choir—whose angels did indeed have a sex: male. These angels, "saw that the daughters of men were fair; and they took to wife such of them as they chose." (Genesis 6:2)

The watchers

In the Old Testament, the Hebrew expression for Grigori is *benej ha'elohim* (sons of God). Grigori, from the Greek, means either "the watchers" or "those who never sleep." The first angels who joined forces with Satanel and turned themselves against God were from this choir, which most closely resembled humans, both physically and mentally. As punishment, they were imprisoned in a sulfurous zone of the fifth Heaven.

Grigori had golden eyes and were giant sized, which predestined them for their primary duties as guards. They also helped the Archangels with the creation of Paradise. According to Enoch, after that two hundred Grigori descended on Mount Hermon (today's Near East) and guarded the people in Paradise.

Due to their proximity to humans, their sexual nature, and their lack of ability to resist temptation, they abandoned themselves to carnal desire. There are old sources that assume up to ninety percent of the Grigori gave in to that desire. Many began to live in close proximity to Eden with human women, and conceived children with them. The women were often held responsible for the angels' indiscretions. One eighth-century rabbi, among others, accused them of going around "showing their nakedness, and painting their eyes with antimony like whores." But the Grigori did more than divert themselves with the women. They also taught them divine secrets, such as mathematics, astronomy, technology, and other aspects of culture, and especially how to make metal weapons and how to prepare perfume.

Nephilim

The offspring of these Grigori and human women are called Nephilim: in Hebrew, *nefil* designates a "mon-

The Grigori were not averse to carnal desire. Their escapades with human women resulted in the Nephilim.

strosity." In the Book of Genesis, we read that "the Nephilim were on the earth in those days, and also afterward, when the sons of God came in to the daughters of men, and they bore children to them. These were the mighty men that were of old, the men of renown." (Genesis 6:4)

"Renown" can also be understood here as "feared," because Nephilim were violent and giant-sized men. Enoch narrated that they terrorized people, and it is also recorded that they enslaved and ate humans. Even the construction of the Tower of Babel, which finally caused the Flood, is attributed to them.

The majority of the Nephilim were extinguished in the Flood, as were the Grigori themselves. Some, however, managed to save themselves, or migrated to Hell.

The most famous Grigori are Semjasa, Urakib, Arameel, Akibeel, Tamiel, Ramuel, Danel, Ezeqeel, Saraqujal, Asael, Armers, Batraal, Anani, Zagebe, Samsaveel, Sartael, Turel, Jomajel, and Sariel.

The Nephilim, too, are supposed to have perished in the Flood.

In the New Testament, Satan is defeated by the most powerful Archangel and driven from Heaven.

ARCHANGELS

Angels and the even more famous Archangels are found in many religions: not only Christianity, Judaism, and Islam, but also among the Aztecs and ancient Egyptians.

The Christian Church limited the number of Archangels to seven by decree, but only designated four by name: Michael, Gabriel, Raphael, and Uriel.

There is ongoing disagreement about the identity of the remaining three Archangels (see box). The seven Archangels—also called the exalted angels—are considered the most important of all angels. They stand before God at the Last Judgment (Revelation 8:2). However, since they are responsible for everything in the divine hierarchy that concerns humanity, these angels appear in the second lowest choir—which is, of course, near to humans.

The number seven is a potent symbol in many faiths. The Bible speaks of God resting on the seventh day of creation, there are seven cardinal virtues and vices, and there are seven heavens and earths in Islam, to mention only a few examples. The Greek philosopher Pythagoras (ca. 570–500 BC) taught that this number is the essence of reality. For the Pythagoreans, seven covers life in its totality: the four elements of the body and the three of the spirit.

Disagreement over the seven

Judaism and Christianity specify that there are seven Archangels, but it is unclear exactly which angels belong to that sublime group.

The apocryphal Old Testament Ethiopian Book of Enoch names the following seven holy angels: Uriel, Raphael, Raguel, Michael, Sariel, Gabriel, and Remiel. In contrast, God is said to have revealed the following names to fifteenth-century Franciscan monk Amadeus Menez de Silva: Michael, Gabriel, Raphael, Uriel, Jehudiel (God's praise), Barachiel (blessing from God), and Sealtiel (prayer of God). These are still accepted today in the Eastern churches, where they are mentioned in many texts and prayers, and Jeremiel/Ramiel (grace of God) is considered an eighth Archangel.

In addition to Michael, Gabriel, and Raphael, the Jewish Talmud still cites the Archangels Anael, Sabbataios (Schepteel), Samael, and Sekiel. This last is believed to have prevented the sacrifice of Isaac.

In the Koran, only four Archangels are mentioned (see page 80 ff), and only two of these are named: Jibril/Jabra'il (Gabriel) and Mika'al (Michael). Two additions to the Islamic Archangels are accepted: Israfil and the giant-sized Izra'il (Azrael). The latter is known as "the angel of death"—when a leaf falls from the Tree of Life, he separates the soul of the human named on the leaf from their body. The similarly larger-than-life-sized Israfil is well-known as the angel of music. His instrument is the sur (horn). On Allah's orders, he will sound it and thus cause the graves to open and the dead to rise.

The Archangel Michael

Michael is the most widely known and highest ranking angel, as well as God's right hand. His Hebrew name means, literally, "who is like God?" Many important actions are attributed to him. It was Michael, for example, who prevented Abraham from sacrificing his son Isaac. In Judaism it is Michael who appeared to Moses as a burning bush, and who parted the Red Sea during the Israelites' exodus from Egypt. According to tradition, Michael is the sword-bearing angel who drove Adam and Eve from Paradise and who guards the Tree of Life. And in the New Testament it is he who defeats the dragon (i.e. Satan) and casts him from Heaven (Revelation 12:7–9). Michael is therefore frequently shown with a bright or flaming sword, often using it to pierce a dragon. Accordingly, it will be Michael, the fighter among the Archangels, who will kill the Anti-Christ after its appearance.

According to Christian belief, Michael is associated with the color red—probably because it is he who creates fire and warmth. Catholics believe that he stands to the east of the throne of God.

The victorious one

In the Book of Daniel it is prophesied that Michael will appear when the world is in desperate need, and in the Middle Ages he was understood to be the angel who leads souls from one realm to the next. Thus, even today, the Catholic church appeals to him in its office for the dead, with the request that "Saint Michael the standard-bearer lead the souls from the pits of Tartarus into holy light." Incidentally, Michael is the only angel that is expressly called an Archangel in the Bible.

An Islamic legend describes how Cherubim are born from Michael's tears as he weeps for the sins of the faithful.

Angel names ending in *el*
All the Archangels' names end in *el*. This is an age-old word that appears in many languages. In Sumerian it means "brightness" or "lights." In Babylonian the word *ellu* stands for "the shining." The syllable also appears in Europe, where the Anglo-Saxon word *aelf* denotes a radiant being. In Hebrew *el* means "God."

The seven Archangels of the Kabbalah
In addition to the great three, the esoteric mystic teachings of the Jewish Kabbalah also mention Haniel (the grace of God), Camael (he who sees God), Zadkiel (righteousness of God) and Tzafkiel (peace of God). In the Kabbalah, the Archangels are assigned to the realm of Hod, or Chod, which means glory and fame.

Michael is considered the fighter among the Archangels.

The feminine characteristics of the angel Gabriel's face are no accident: this angel is seen as the only female heavenly messenger.

The Archangel Gabriel

The Archangel Gabriel (Arabic *Jibril*) holds a special place in the angelic throng, being seen as the only feminine angel (and hence sometimes called Gabrielle). In works of art, this Archangel (and only this one) is often shown with feminine facial features and attributes. In the Hebrew, the name means "God is my strength." The Sumerian root of the name means guide, helmsman, and also governor. But Gabriel can also mean "divine spouse," a translation that fits the story in the Gospel of Luke (and the Koran), in which Gabriel was the one who announced to Mary that she would conceive Christ (in the Gospel of Matthew, it was the Holy Spirit). The traditional belief that Gabriel fetches souls from Paradise and prepares them for life on Earth during the nine months of pregnancy is a further aspect of this angel's lore that supports the conviction that Gabriel is a female angel.

The female Archangel

Gabriel is invoked frequently in connection with all aspects of generation and birth, and is the logical patron against conjugal barrenness. In Christian and Jewish belief, Gabriel is the head of the Cherubim and Seraphim, and Catholic doctrine places him on the north side of the throne of God. In the Catholic church, Gabriel is depicted with a lily. Gabriel is the manager of Eden and assigned the color blue. This may be based on the early Christian understanding, according to which Gabriel has dominion over the element of water.

Gabriel is an important messenger in several faiths. Jewish legends relate that it was Gabriel who spoke to Noah, allowing him to escape the Flood. He prophesied the coming of the Messiah to Daniel (Daniel 9:20 ff), the birth of John the Baptist to Zacharias (Luke 1:11–19), and the arrival of Jesus Christ to the shepherds (Luke 2:9). According to Islam, Jibril (that is, Gabriel) dictated the Koran to Mohammed, one sutra at a time (see page 80), and accompanied Mohammed into the heavens. In Islamic lore, Gabriel is named *Ruh al-qudus*—Holy Spirit.

The Archangel Raphael

Raphael is the guardian angel of the Tree of Life in the Garden of Eden.

As is made clear by his name, Archangel Raphael is the healing angel. Hebrew *rapha'el* or *raphach* means "God heals (the soul)." In the Old Testament Raphael is mentioned by name only in the Book of Tobit (Tobias), in which Raphael protected the traveling Tobit from the demon Aschmodai, but did not allow himself to be recognized as an Archangel (Tobit 5). The fact that Raphael is an adept of the healing arts emerges when an enormous fish frightens Tobit near the Tigris River. Together they catch it and on Raphael's advice Tobit removes the gall bladder, liver and heart, which later prove to be medicine.

According to Enoch (First Book of Enoch, see box, page 9), Raphael is one of the four angels who help in times of need; he "is set over all the diseases and all the wounds of the children of men."

The physician

It is difficult to classify Raphael into a triad. Officially he belongs to the Powers, although he has the six wings of the Seraphim. He is also considered a Cherubim and a Dominion. He is a regent of the sun, second governing prince of the second Heaven, most powerful of the Powers, guardian angel of the Tree of Life in the Garden of Eden and, by his own statement in the Book of Tobit, one of the seven Throne angels who stand in the presence of God according to the Jewish faith. As a healing angel Raphael is often shown with the caduceus (symbol of the healing professions) or a medicine bottle. He is believed to have conveyed all texts on healing, as well as the emerald tablet of Hermes Trismegistos. Raphael gave the Book of Raziel to Noah, who built the ark with its help. All who serve science and medicine belong to Raphael's angelic legions. He is a protective patron of travelers, physicians, and pharmacists.

Raphael protects Tobit from a demon and introduces him to the secrets of the healing arts.

The Archangel Uriel

The Archangel Uriel is both Seraph and Cherub. Despite his Hebrew name, which means "God is my light" or "fire of God," Uriel is one of the darkest angels in Heaven. In the eighth century, a church council banished him to Hell, but he was later rehabilitated purely on account of his name. Today Uriel is seen as the master of order. He punishes human injustices and is overseer of Tartarus (Hell). In the Ethiopian Book of Enoch (see page 9, box) it is written that Uriel locks the abyss where the fallen angels are imprisoned. He promotes repentance and hope in those who will inherit eternal life.

As a fiery serpent he once attacked Moses for failing to circumcise his son. The dark angel who wrestled with Jacob was also Uriel. He watches over thunder and lightning, and stands with fiery sword at the gate of the Garden of Eden. In the Apocalypse of Peter, he is the avenging angel of atonement and on the Day of Judgment, he will open the gates of Hell to lead sinners before God and burn them and their houses in an eternal fire.

With flaming sword Uriel guards the entrance to the Garden of Eden.   As the dark angel, Uriel wrestles with Jacob.

The dark angel

But merciful and illuminating acts are also attributed to Uriel, one of the four angels constantly in the presence of God. He is said to have given the magic Kabbalah to humans and to have warned Noah before the Flood.

Uriel is also well-known as Auriel and Phanuel ("face of God"). He is not mentioned by name in the Bible, although he does appear in the apocryphal Fourth Book of Ezra, which some Orthodox churches recognize as canonical. There, he leads Ezra through Heaven and Hell. In the Catholic view, he stands on the south side of God's throne. His color is silvery white.

The Archangel Raguel

This name can be interpreted as "friend of God" or "divine companion." Like Uriel, this angel was expunged from the liturgical calendar by Pope Zacharias (741–752) in the eighth-century church council. Raguel is mentioned in the apocryphal Revelation of John the Theologian, in which this angel is commanded to "sound the trumpet for the angels of cold and snow and ice."

The judge

According to the apocryphal Ethiopian Book of Enoch, Raguel—who is also known by the names Rasuil, Rufael, and Akrasiel—watches over "the world of luminaries" (or, more precisely, over the behavior of the angels). The role of the judiciary falls to him, while the Archangel Sariel represents the executive. Enoch, whom Raguel transported into Heaven, adds the following description: "Raguel, one of the holy angels who takes vengeance on the world of the luminaries." In this case, luminaries refers to angels who have committed transgressions.

Raguel, who is often represented with a trumpet, judges the misdeeds of the angels.

Remiel is believed to have destroyed the army of the Assyrian King Sanherib during the siege of Jerusalem.

The Archangel Remiel

Also known as Jeremiel (see page 48, box), Ramiel or Yerahmeel, this Seraph's name translates as "grace of God." Like Uriel, he is sometimes also called Phanuel (face of God).

As an angel of the resurrection, Remiel protects the souls of the righteous after their death until the point in time when they will enter Heaven. Therefore he is also denoted as the lord of souls that await the resurrection. He is sent by God to lead them to the Last Judgment. According to the Book of Enoch, he is additionally responsible for transmitting orders to the seven Archangels.

Lord of souls

Remiel's most famous deed dates to the year 701 BC. In a single night, he (and not the Archangel Michael, as claimed in some quarters) destroyed the 185,000-strong army of the Assyrian king Sanherib, who had besieged Jerusalem. In the process, Remiel overcame the pagan god Nisroch, who had received an eagle's

head at the time he was deified, and was also known as "Great Eagle." King Sanherib was killed by his sons in the temple of Nisroch in the ancient Mesopotamian city of Nineveh in 681 BC.

In 1667, the poet and philosopher John Milton (1608–1674) published his epic poem, *Paradise Lost*, in which Nisroch appears as a leader of the fallen angels. The poem tells the story of the fall of Adam and Eve and of their expulsion from the Garden of Eden.

Along with Uriel and Salathiel, Remiel is mentioned in the Latin and Slavic versions of the Book of Ezra. The Archangel Remiel is also responsible for genuine visions.

Remiel protects the souls of the deceased until the time of their entry into Heaven—in this representation he does so in the company of some other angels.

Angels battle with demons—which side is Sariel on? Depending on the source, he is seen as either a good angel or a fallen one.

The Archangel Sariel

Sariel is also known as Suriel, Suriyel, Zerachiel, and Saraquel. His name can be interpreted as "God's command." This is a direct reference to his role as the strong arm of God in relation to the angelic hosts. If Raguel exercises the judiciary function in Heaven, then Sariel is the executive. He is the angel of death, and his sphere of activity is therefore limited to a single duty. In the Book of Enoch he is denoted as the one responsible for the fate of angels who have transgressed the law. Thus he punishes those who break divine laws or neglect their duties.

In contrast with this role, Sariel's calling also concerns health. He differs from Raphael in that he is particularly concerned with matters of cleanliness and hygiene, rather than healing. He has repeatedly passed on this knowledge to people. Thus he is said to have instructed Moses, although this is also attributed to Zagzagel, the angel of wisdom.

The angel of death

It remains unclear whether Sariel, Seraph and prince of the inner circle, should be seen as a fallen angel or a son of light. The Book of Enoch lists him (and also Remiel) among the rebel angels. In fact, Sariel is even named as their leader. In a painting attributed to the Italian artist Francesco Traini (1321–1363), Sariel is depicted with the wings of a demon; yet at the great battle of the sons of light against the sons of darkness, he is listed on the side of those who fight on the side of the light, with his name appearing on the shields of a unit.

According to some sources, Metatron is seen as the most powerful Archangel—others, however, equate him with the Archangel Michael.

The Archangel Metatron

The Archangel Metatron was formerly the prophet and scholar Enoch on Earth (not to be confused with Enoch, son of Cain) and father of Methuselah. He visited Heaven several times and served as the divine scribe, recorder of truth, before he was transformed into a Seraph with thirty-six wings and 365 eyes, each as bright as the sun. His age is said to be approximately 8,500 years. His name is also unusual—it has no meaning in any well-known language.

In Judaism, Metatron is considered the king of the angels and chancellor of Heaven. He provides for food on Earth and manifests God's will. Following his victory over the Egyptian magicians he rose even above Michael and Gabriel in rank. The Jewish Talmud and the Aramaic Targum see him as a direct link between humanity and God.

Further names for this most powerful Archangel are "angel of the covenant," "angel of the face," "angel of the presence," and "lesser Yahweh."

The mightiest of all

In the Second Book of Moses, Metatron leads with an iron hand; he is vindictive and deals cruelly with his people. He appears as column of fire and as a burning thorn bush, and his face shines more brightly than the sun.

Despite his exalted position and tremendous power, his duty continues to be that of divine scribe, recording everything that happens in the divine archives.

Metatron, who is not only the most powerful but also the tallest of the angels, has an especially important role in relation to the people of Israel: according to *Zohar*—the most important book of the esoteric teachings of the Kabbalah—it was Metatron who led the people of Israel during their exodus from Egypt.

Metatron is not mentioned in Christian or Islamic sources, and is equated with Michael in some spheres.

The Archangel Raziel recorded the 1500 secrets of the universe in a book that aided Adam, Enoch, Noah, and Solomon.

The Archangel Raziel

The Archangel Raziel is a Cherub and is viewed by Moses Maimonides (1138–1204)—the most important Jewish scholar of the Middle Ages—as head of the Thrones, among other things. He is also known by the names of Ratziel, Gallizur, Saraquel, and Akrasiel. His name literally means "secrets of God" or "knowledge of the divine."

The book of 1500 secrets

In the Jewish mystical tradition, Raziel is thought to stay very near to God and record all that happens around his throne; even the angels cannot understand what he has written, so mysterious is the language he used. The most important deed by this angel of the secrets and highest mysteries is writing the Book of Raziel, which is believed to contain all earthly and heavenly knowledge. This work has traveled long and far through human history. In Paradise it was conferred on Adam to enable him to look into the mirror of

The Archangel Metatron is seen as the archivist of Heaven, and as a cruel and vindictive ruler.

reality and see the divine face there; that is, himself as the image of God.

Raziel's book was later given to Enoch, who transcribed part of it into its own work. In the same book, Noah found instructions for building the ark. The book was also associated with Solomon, and later still with Eleazar of Worms in Germany. The 1500 keys to the secrets of the universe are thought to be revealed in the Book of Raziel—but it was evidently written in the language of the angels and can no longer be decoded.

The Aramaic Targum, one of the first translations of the Bible, recounts that Raziel stands on the highest peak of Mount Horeb promulgating divine secrets of the world, day after day. The Archangel Raziel is also mentioned in the Pirke Rabbi Eliesar, a Jewish book of mysteries attributed to Rabbi Eliesar and once thought to have been written in the first century (although more recent studies assume that it is a collection of eighth-century texts). It is Raziel who stands before the heavenly throne and spreads his wings over the Hayyoth, living creatures of the same rank as Cherubim, to prevent their fiery breath from scorching the angels. Raziel is recognizable as a bright white fire.

THE DARK SIDE
OF ANGELS

On the second day of creation the first great battle between good and evil took place.

THE WAR OF THE ANGELS

The War of the Angels—the first great battle between good and evil—took place on the second day of God's creation. Enoch was the first to write about the angelic rebellion, and he named two hundred rebels. In the thirteenth century, however, the bishop of Tusculum

numbered 133,306,668 rebel angels, which is one third of the entire angel host.

The catalyst for the war was Lucifer, who refused to pay homage to humans, and wanted to occupy God's throne, as well.

A fiery red dragon with seven heads

In the War of the Angels, Lucifer and his adherents fought against Michael and the angels loyal to God, as can be read in Revelation: "Now war arose in Heaven, Michael and his angels fighting against the dragon; and the dragon and his angels fought, but they were defeated and there was no longer any place for them in Heaven. And the great dragon was thrown down, that ancient serpent, who is called the Devil and Satan, the deceiver of the whole world—he was thrown down to the earth, and his angels were thrown down with him." (Revelation 12:7–9) Just before this, it says: "And another portent appeared in Heaven; behold, a great red dragon, with seven heads and ten horns, and seven diadems upon his heads. His tail swept down a third of the stars of Heaven, and cast them to the earth." The dragon is Lucifer, and the stars stand for the angels, one third of whom followed Lucifer. Michael ultimately defeated Lucifer and cast him from Heaven. Revelation then gives his new name: the Adversary (Hebrew *Satan*).

It is fitting that the last sentence that Lucifer is said to have heard in Heaven before he was banished was "Who is like God?"—which is the ancient meaning of the name Michael.

The narrative of Lucifer has strong parallels with the legend of the Canaanite god of the (red) dawn, Shaher. He, too, was the morning star of Heaven who heralded the rising sun. Shaher tried to conquer the sun's throne of light and was cast out of the heavenly realm for that reason.

Gehenna

Satan, too, fell from this heavenly realm. He landed in Hell, far from the love and light of God. The original name for this place in the Old Testament is Gehenna (also Gehinnom or Geena, which is Greek). This can be roughly translated as "valley of Hinnom." This valley, southwest of Jerusalem, is an actual place where the Ammonites are believed to have sacrificed children to their god Moloch in the dim and distant past. During the first century AD, the corpses of criminals were cremated in the ravine, which was also used as a dump. This corresponds to the traditional image of hell fire. A further name for Hell is Sheol.

The name Hell derives from the old Germanic *hel*, the name for the underworld where the dragon Nidhögg eats the corpses of law breakers.

Seven plagues at the end of time

Hell is not the homeland of Satanel and the other fallen angels, but he dwells there. Satanel tries to divert as many humans as possible from the right path, both by means of lies and seduction, and by minimizing, concealing, or hindering missionary work.

The first War of the Angels was not yet the decisive battle—this will take place before the Last Judgment. For a short while beforehand, evil will take over the world, false prophets will emerge, and love will grow cold, as it says in the Gospel of Matthew. According to Revelation, the seven plagues of the end time can then be expected. These are boils, sea water turning into blood, fresh water becoming blood, a heat wave, darkness, drying up of all sources of water, and the greatest earthquake in history.

Eternal Paradise—eternal damnation

At the end of this time of horror, the sun will darken, the moon will no longer shine, and the stars will fall

The Apocalypse of John
The last book of the Bible, Revelation, is equally well-known as the Apocalypse of John. It is the only book of the New Testament that is exclusively prophetic. The Apocalypse treats the end of time as we know it and leads to the expectation of a "new earth," in which all people will live in the presence of God.

According to the Apocalypse of John, the ultimate and decisive battle between the forces of good and evil will take place before the Last Judgment.

from the heavens. When this occurs, the dead will rise and the Last Judgment will take place, with Jesus Christ as judge.

At this time (according to the prophecy of John), the legions of Hell will be defeated by those of Heaven under the leadership of the Archangel Michael. The defeated angels—along with human beings, both the living and dead—will then be sorted. Afterwards, according to the Catholic faith, some will be condemned to everlasting punishment in Hell. Sinful humans will land in a lake of fire and brimstone. The others will inherit a newly created and paradisiac world of eternal life. Sects that take the Bible literally believe that Jesus will establish a thousand-year realm upon his return. During that time Satan will be bound. Afterwards he will be released again to tempt humanity—in a kind of final trial—and will ultimately be brought back to the lake of fire. Only then, according to Revelation, will the resurrection of the dead take place.

VINCE TEIPSVM.

Johann Weyer was an opponent of witch hunting and wrote a detailed treatise on Hell.

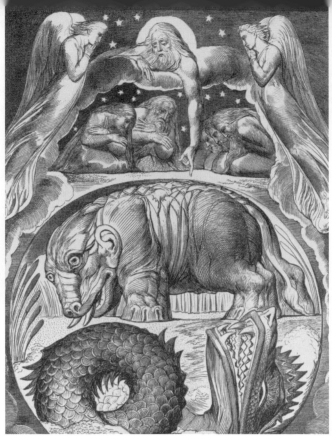

Leviathan—the dragon of chaos—resides in Hell, too. Here he is represented in his capacity as Behemoth.

THE INHABITANTS OF HELL

Perhaps the most significant work on the hierarchy of Hell came from Johann Weyer. He was probably born in 1515 in Grave-an-der-Maas, Holland, and was the son of a merchant. This physician wrote several medical treatises and was an avowed opponent of the persecution of witches. In 1577 he published the text *Pseudomonarchia Daemonium* (False Kingdom of Demons). This was preceded in 1563 by the book *De praestigiis daemonum* (On the Illusion of the Demons). This became very popular; it was reprinted several times and also translated into several languages. But it was also added to the list of forbidden books, and alleged experts on witches and witchcraft (such as Jean Bodin and Martin Anton) spoke out against the book. Nevertheless, Weyer's work did lead to fewer death sentences and was the standard reference for every opponent of witch trials. For Weyer, the alleged witches were victims of the Devil, who led them astray and left them mentally ill. In his opinion, they needed medical treatment above all and did not under any circumstances merit death.

7,405,926 demons

Pseudomonarchia Daemonium describes the structure of Hell, which is arranged according to a strict hierarchy. Like the Jewish Talmud, Weyer's work assumes there are a total of 7,405,926 demons, divided into seventy-two companies. Johann Weyer lists the chief demons, their titles, their appearance, and the number of their subordinate legions.

This probably served as a source of information for the *Ars Goetia*, the first part of *The Lesser Key of Solomon*, a book of magic also known as the *Lemegeton*. The *Goetia* describes the seventy-two demons that King Solomon is said to have conjured and then held captive in a bronze vessel. It also contains complicated instructions on how to achieve this. The famous English author and occultist Aleister Crowley (1875–1947) published *Ars Goetia* in English in 1904, editing it at the same time.

In Weyer's *Pseudomonarchia Daemonium*, Beelzebub is denoted as the supreme lord of Hell and founder of

Demons risk everything to lead people into temptation. Female demons are well-known for their seductive skill.

Female demons

In addition to Lilith (see page 70), there are other female inhabitants of Hell on record. With her, Agrat-Bat-Mahlaht, Eisheth-Zenunim, and Naamah are listed as the four "whore angels," and all are at the same time brides of Satan. Naamah is the most erotic and thus the most skillful seductress. She is thought to have been the sister of Tubal Kain, the original father of all goldsmiths and blacksmiths, as well as Noah.

The archdemoness Barbelo is also described as beautiful, immaculate, and even brighter than God himself. The great female dragon of chaos, Leviathan (Hebrew for coiled one), is considered an archdemoness. She shines so brightly that her shafts of light obliterate the sun. According to the Old Testa-ment, God created the Leviathan "as a play fellow." The Babylonian Talmud records that he did this in the last three hours of the day. Job (41:15–31) describes this creature in great detail: *His back is made of rows of shields [scales], shut up closely as with a seal ... Out of his mouth go flaming torches; sparks of fire leap forth ... When he raises himself up the mighty are afraid ... He makes the deep boil like a pot..."* According to the Bible, God will "crush the head" of Leviathan, whose flesh will then be given to the righteous for food.

Proserpina, the archdemoness, originally derived from Greek mythology. Hades abducted Persephone, the daughter of Zeus and Demeter, and made her his wife in the underworld.

the Order of the Fly. The great subordinate leaders are: Satan (Prince of Darkness, The Adversary), Pluto (Prince of Fire and Hades), Molech (Prince of the Vale of Tears), Baal (General of the Demonic Army), Lucifer (Highest Judge), Baal-Beryth (Minister of Bargains and Pacts with the Devil), Nergal (Prince of the Secret Police), Proserpina (Greek: Persephone, archdemoness, see box), as well as Astaroth (Treasurer of Hell).

fourteen faces, and twelve wings. He is thought to have been one of the Cherubim at one time, but is now a desert demon and the head flag bearer of Hell's legions. On the Jewish Day of Atonement (Yom Kippur) it is Azazel, in the form of a goat (the "scapegoat"), who bears away the sins of the world.

Azazel was also a teacher of people before he gave in to desire. His gifts included the manufacture and use of weapons, jewelry and mirrors, as well as make-up; but he also gave them secret heavenly knowledge. The Archangel Raphael stoned him for his sins and banished him into the darkness. In the First Book of Enoch is the following passage: "And on the day of the great judgment he shall be cast into the fire … And the whole earth has been corrupted through the works that were taught by Azazel: to him ascribe all sin."

Some sources consider Azazel and Sammael to be a single spirit, but there are also records that view Sammael (poison of God) as a fallen Seraph. He is supposed to be married to Lilith (see page 70) and was in former times seen as the guardian angel of Rome—which for the early Hebrews was the source of all evil.

The scapegoat

The inhabitants of Hell also include the angels of the tenth angelic choir who did not land in the prison of the third Heaven. The sources name two leaders of the Grigori in Hell—Azazel and Semjaza (or Semyaza; serpent)—although Semjaza is occasionally also described as a Seraph. Semjaza's crime was that he betrayed God's secret name for the beautiful Ishtar. Enoch names Semjaza as chief leader of the angels who slept with human women. Before his betrayal, he is said to have taught people the art of evocation and cutting roots.

The other possible leader of this group of fallen angels in Hell is Azazel, who has seven serpent heads,

The angels on one side and the demons on the other struggle for the souls of humans.

Even in Hell there is a hierarchy—the highest spirits are known as the seven Princes of Hell, who manage the hordes of devils.

The seven princes of Hell

It was not only the Grigori, but also other angels as well, who fell to Hell. Thus the seven princes of Hell include Baal-Beryth, Sariel, Mephistopheles, Rofocal, Meririm, Rahab and Dumah.

Baal-Beryth, the "Federal Lord," was once a prince of the Cherubim. Now he is responsible for all demonic ceremonies and sets his name on all pacts with mortal humans.

According to *Zohar* (the core work of the Kabbalah), Dumah, "silence of death," is the chief prince of Hell.

Mephistopheles, "light hater" or "stench lover," is thought to have been an Archangel before the Fall. This prince of Hell is known for his slippery tongue and his philosophical bent.

It is not known which angelic choir the demonic prince Rofocal once belonged to. His field of responsibility includes all earthly treasures. He is also dedicated as the chancellor of Hell.

Hellish prince Meririm is considered "the angel of the Apocalypse." His role consists of cursing both the continents and all the seas. The apostle Paul denotes him as the prince of air—a title that is held only by Meririm and Satan.

Although the Greek word *raab* means "rave," the prince of Hell Rahab is not famous for his irascible nature, but for his insolence and pride. He was banished to Hell by God after he refused to divide the waters, a task that fell to him as angel of the primordial sea.

Sariel is the contradictory angel: he is known as both an Archangel (see page 55) and a Grigori. In some sources he is listed as a prince of Hell. His crime is supposed to have been passing on secret knowledge. Canaanite priestesses are thought to have learned the phases of the moon and tides from him.

In addition to the princes of Hell there are archdemons, punishing angels, and dukes of Hell, among whose ranks are God's spies, such as the angel Zaphiel.

LUCIFER

A deeper fall than that of the angel Lucifer (Latin for "light bearer") is hardly conceivable. He was not just any angel, but the first Seraph created by God, the most magnificent of all angels. Ezekiel (28:12–15) narrates, "You were the signet of perfection, full of wisdom and perfect in beauty." A list of all the jewels with which he was covered follows: "every precious stone was your covering, carnelian, topaz, and jasper, chrysolite, beryl, and onyx, sapphire, carbuncle, and emerald; and wrought in gold were your settings and your engravings." Lucifer was flawless—until he sinned.

He was also well-known as Son of the Morning, Prince of the Air, and a regent of God (thus his deputy). Lucifer was the original name of the morning star, Venus. The twelve-winged Lucifer should have brought wisdom and illumination to humanity.

Before his fall, Satan was called Lucifer, and was the most splendid of the Archangels. As God's adversary, he tried to lead Jesus into temptation.

The fall of Lucifer

The reason for Lucifer's fall from grace is disputed. The most familiar charge cites Lucifer's refusal to honor the man, Adam. It was his opinion that as an angel he need honor only God, and that humans ranked below angels. "How can a son of fire bow before a son of earth?" Lucifer is supposed to have asked God.

In addition, it is related that Lucifer sat on the heavenly throne in God's absence. By doing so, he sought to make himself equal to God. This is described in the Book of Isaiah (Isaiah 14:13–14): "You said in your heart, 'I will ascend to Heaven; above the stars of God I will set my throne on high; I will sit on the mount of assembly in the far north; I will ascend above the heights of the clouds, I will make myself like the Most High.'"

Afterwards, Lucifer was cast from Heaven, either by God or, alternatively, by the Archangel Michael during the War of the Angels (see page 49). In Isaiah (14:12) it may also be read, "How you are fallen from Heaven, O Day Star, son of Dawn!"

Luke 10:18 states, "And he said to them, I saw Satan fall like lightning from Heaven." Through this fall, Lucifer became Satanel, the dragon of the dawn. In Hebrew *Satan* means "to plot against" or "the adversary." Satan is known by many names, including Sammael, Mastema, Beliel, Azazel, Beelzebub, Duma, Gadeel, Sier, Samael, Mephistopheles, and Asmodeus, although several authorities assume that at least some of these names represent independent spirits.

An additional series of names resulted from the long-held belief that it was unlucky to speak the Devil's name out loud. These include the Great Dragon, the Serpent, the Evil One, the Anti-Christ, the Prince of Darkness, the Archfiend, the Prince of Hell, and the Tempter.

Ever since his fall, Lucifer has acted as God's adversary, as the inversion of all that is good and all that proceeds from God. In Hell he gathered not only the fallen angels, but also the damned souls around him. In Satanel all seven deadly sins are united: pride, envy, wrath, sloth, avarice, gluttony, and lust. He is frequently depicted with horns, a hooked nose, hairy legs, and cloven hooves. Thus he is outwardly similar to the Greek shepherd god Pan. As Satanel, Lucifer has only six wings instead of twelve.

In Hell Satan reigns over the fallen angels and damned souls.

Devil worship

During the fifteenth to eighteenth centuries—the time of widespread witch hunts in Europe—witches and wizards were accused of making pacts with Satanel, or even of having had sex with him (which was a sign of Devil worship).

Authorities do not all assume that Lucifer will continue to be Satanel for all of eternity. Saint Jerome states that one day Lucifer will again take his place in Heaven.

In Islam, Satanel is known as Shaitaan or Iblis. However, he is not an angel but a jinn (see box, pages 82–83), a demon who deceives humans in order to make them choose between him and God. This is one of the ways humans are tested. Thus Shaitaan is a mere tool of Allah and not all-powerful. Shaitaan, too, was originally the leader of all the angels.

LUCIFER IN THE VISIONS OF JAKOB LORBER

Jakob Lorber, musician and mystic.

The Austrian musician and mystic Jakob Lorber (1800–1864) was just about to take up his duties as bandmaster in the town of Trieste on March 15, 1840, when he heard a voice for the first time that would continue to speak to him for the next twenty-four years. Lorber described these messages as follows: "Concerning the internal word, as one hears the same, I, speaking of myself, can say only that I hear the Lord's holy word always in the area of the heart like a most clear thought, light and pure, like expressed words. Nobody, no matter how close to me they stand, can hear any voice at all. For me, however, this merciful voice rings out more brightly than any audible sound, no matter how loud it might be."

When Lorber heard the voice for the first time it commanded him, "Take up your pen and write!"

Lorber duly did so. What was dictated to him by the voice would become a vast enterprise over the years, comprising twenty-five books altogether, as well as many smaller works. Lorber coined his own name for himself, "the scribe of God."

Science for the next century

Writing down what he heard did not make Lorber a wealthy man by any means. On the contrary, it led to a meager life. His original manuscripts are still in existence, and it is clear that they were never corrected or revised. The voice dictated religious and also scientific texts containing material that was not yet known in the nineteenth century. These writings, Lorber was informed, were not intended for the people of his century, but for those of the next. Today it is known that the texts also contain some scientific errors that do not support the claim that an all-knowing God was their source.

But the religious writings, recognized by Lorber's devotees as the "New Revelation," were and remain the more important ones. The most extensive and most famous work is *The Great Gospel of John* in ten volumes. This supplements the Gospel of John and describes how his gospel should be understood.

Lorber's body of writings also includes detailed passages on the meaning of the fall of Lucifer. In them it is explained that he was the first angel created by God, and that Lucifer then went on to create all the other angels in turn. When Lucifer rebelled, however, God was reluctant to destroy him because that would also have meant the destruction of all the angels Lucifer had created, including those who remained loyal to God. So God chose another way instead: he created the material world. This serves a single purpose only, which is to give Lucifer and all the other fallen angels the opportunity to return to God of their own free will.

Lorber—also known as "God's scribe"—took dictation from a divine inner voice for many years.

The Earth as a path to God

The internal voice also dictated the following to Lorber: "For this, then, the material world was created. In it the spirits were wrapped in matter according to the degree of their malevolence and endure struggle, temptation, and suffering—primarily, to move them gradually into an understanding of their own error by introducing the conditions caused by it, and thus, secondly, to move them to repentance of their own free will. The whole visible creation consists only of particles of the great fallen and the matter-bound spirits of Lucifer and his followers. I tell you, neither the Earth, nor the sun, nor any material thing would ever have been created, were not this the only remaining way to humble them."

According to the divine scribe, one day, all fallen angels will return to God by way of the detour of this material world. The world will then have served its purpose and cease to exist. There will "no longer be a material sun and a material Earth circling in endless space, but everywhere a glorious new spiritual creation with blessed free spirits filling the unlimited space." This state will be eternal.

Before God created Eve, Adam had a first wife: Lilith, who later
became Lucifer's favorite playmate.

LILITH

According to ancient lore in several traditions, Eve was
not Adam's original mate. That was Lilith, who, according to the Jewish Talmud, God created from the dust
of the ground. Her Hebrew name means "spirit of the
night." She was not only beautiful, but also wild (in the
sense of untamed) and temperamental. Adam insisted
that she have sex with him in the missionary position,
that is, lying underneath him. As the first emancipated
woman she saw no reason why she, too, should not be
on top—after all, she was made from the same dust
as Adam.

Some orthodox Jews, Christians, and Muslims,
however, deplore this as contemptible. In Islam one
finds the statement "cursed be the man who makes the
woman the heaven and himself the earth."

In the Bible, although Lilith is not specifically
named as Adam's original mate, Genesis indirectly
implies her existence. It is written in Genesis 1:27,
"So God created man in his own image, in the image
of God he created him; male and female he created
them." Only later, in Genesis 2:18–23, was Eve created
from Adam's rib.

Adam's original mate

The reason for Lilith's rebellion is supposedly the fact that the dust from which she was created was poisoned with the spittle of the banished angel Samael.

After a disagreement, Lilith left Adam. She then successfully used her magic to summon God by uttering his true name. This knowledge gave her immense power and she demanded wings, which she also received from God.

Her banishment followed, nevertheless, and Lilith landed in Hell, where she became one of the four brides of Satan himself, his beloved playmate. She bore the Prince of Hell one hundred beautiful female demons who are called the lilim. Other sources claim that when she was exiled from Paradise she went into the desert or wilderness where she copulates with a thousand demons a day, thus bringing a thousand evil spirits into the world every day. Isaiah 34:14 states, "And wild beasts shall meet with hyenas, the satyr shall cry to his fellow; yea, there shall the night hag [Lilith] alight, and find for herself a resting place."

The lilim (the whores of Hell mentioned above) also copulate with men as they sleep—an idea that is particularly problematic for clergymen. The lilim prefer the same position as their mother, Lilith, in which they squat on top of the man. Monks used to fasten crosses to their penises to protect them from the lilim. A man who has once been seduced by lilim can never again love a woman.

Manifestation of lust

Their mother Lilith is considered the "Queen of the Night," the manifestation of lust, and also the embodiment of deception and seduction, since she can cause men to obsess on carnal desire. Over time, however, Lilith assumed demonic characteristics and her beauty vanished.

In the Jewish religion, there are legends of the ten unholy Sephiroth, of whom Lilith may be one. Since the angels Sanvai, Sansanvi, and Semangloph once pursued the Sephiroth on God's behalf, talismans with their portraits are used to protect infants from being murdered (the Talmud also invokes a protective charm against Lilith). In fact, the three missionary angels

As "Queen of the Night" Lilith lives in Hell and is the mother of hundreds or even thousands of beautiful demonesses.

actually found Lilith and tried to persuade her to return to Adam. Only when Lilith refused did God create Eve.

Critical texts see Lilith as the remnant of a rabbinical attempt to integrate the Babylonian goddess Belet-ili into the structure of the Jewish faith. The "holy lady" was well-known to the Canaanites by the name of Ba'alat, and was also addressed as Lillake. The Hebrew name Lilith could be derived from Babylonian Lilitu, which means wind spirit.

ADDITIONAL CONCEPTS OF ANGELS

Angels escort the soul of a deceased man into Heaven.

Emanuel Swedenborg, scientist and mystic.

EMANUEL SWEDENBORG'S
VISIONS OF ANGELS

One of the most extensive and most unusual conceptions of the existence of the angels comes from the Swedish scientist, mystic, visionary, and theologian Emanuel Swedenborg (1688–1772). He studied in Sweden, then traveled to France, the Netherlands, and Germany and stayed in London for several years. He was a student of Isaac Newton and Edmond Hailey. For thirty years he enjoyed a career as a renowned scientist and wrote around 150 publications on topics including mathematics, mineralogy, chemistry, astronomy, anatomy and psychology. Thus Swedenborg was an all-round scholar when, at the age of 56, he finally

began to analyze his own dreams. By his own account, he very quickly experienced visions, which ultimately charged him with a commission: he was to expound the secret meaning of the holy writ and describe the spirits from Heaven and Hell for all people.

Conversations with the angels and the dead

Thereafter, Swedenborg learned to communicate with angels and spirits, and also with the dead; he lived, as he expressed it, on Earth and in Heaven simultaneously. One result is that Swedenborg had access to prophetic knowledge. One convincing example of this occured on July 19, 1759. Swedenborg provided a detailed description of a city fire that was raging in his hometown of Stockholm, which was some 250 miles (400 km) away from Göteborg, where Swedenborg was at the time.

Written exclusively in Latin, his texts include very clear descriptions of angels and demons. The central work in this area bears the name *Heaven and Hell*.

Swedenborg's work formed the basis for the New Church (also known as the Church of the New Jerusalem). In 1788, the London suburb of Great Eastcheap became the first public municipality formed according to Swedenborgian precepts.

Swedenborg's concept of the world is based on the soul. In his opinion, this is the essence of a person. The body is nothing more than an organ by means of which humans are able to exist in the material world. Death means simply the transition of the essential person (soul) from one world to the next—something Swedenborg understood as an awakening. In this transition, people enter the so-called spirit world, where spirits lovingly familiarize the newly deceased with their new existence.

Every person has the freedom to choose whether to follow the spirits of Heaven or those of Hell. However, their final destination has already been chosen through the kind of life they led on Earth.

Angel or demon?

Those who choose good become angels, while choosing the dark side results in existence as a demon. From that time forward, the latter will eternally torment themselves and each other. There are no angels or demons who were originally created as such: all of them were originally people.

Two factors that characterize Emanuel Swedenborg's concept of Heaven are his own unique dynamism and his emphasis on the individuality of each angel. As understood by Swedenborg, the heavenly world is like a continual flow, caught up in endless change. The reason for this is the evolution of the angels, who are constantly striving to further perfect themselves.

According to Swedenborg, everyone chooses freely whether to follow the spirits of Heaven or Hell. The decisive factor is each person's behavior during life.

In Heaven, the angels live in palaces of gold and precious gems, given to them by God.

With the eyes of the spirit

By Swedenborg's account, angels are completely human in form. They can see and hear, they talk with one another, they write texts. Their difference from humans lies in the fact that they are "not clothed in a material body." They are light spirits in solid form. However, they radiate a light that is brighter than day.

Swedenborg says one cannot see angels with the eyes of the human body, but only with the eyes of the spirit, as the physical body is located in the natural world. On the other hand, Swedenborg's spirit is also thought to have traveled to the spirit world.

As a result of these journeys, he claimed it was possible for him to describe Heaven in detail from his own observation. However, the descriptions thus gained are purely metaphorical, even allegoric, in order to make them comprehensible to people who only know the physical world.

Palaces of gold and gems

According to Swedenborg, every angel is clothed in accordance with the kind and degree of its divine understanding.

Those with greater understanding are more beautifully clothed than others. The weakest understanding is reflected in multicolored clothes, followed in ascending order by plain or dazzling white. Great insight is reflected in a fiery glow. "The angels of the innermost heaven appear naked, because they are innocent, and nakedness corresponds to innocence," says Swedenborg.

The angels live in palaces, which shine above like pure gold, and below like jewels. Inside, everything is embellished with decorations. An angel's palace is an image of the goodness of its owner; thus the interior details correspond to the details of the owner's goodness. Everything outside of these dwellings reflects the truth that comes from God. Thus there is no material wealth that could be acquired. Furthermore, the houses are not built, but are given by God. Indeed, they change as their inhabitants change.

The angels in Swedenborg's visions have been given duties to fulfill in Heaven: the care of small children, the education of adolescents, the proselytizing of pagans, and the protection of spiritual novices, to mention only a few. Some angels are also sent to people to alert them to wrong tendencies. But the Devil sends his minions to humans in the same way. Thus people gain absolute balance and especially the opportunity to choose freely between good and evil.

The language of the angels

The angels have their own language, which does not have to be learned. The sounds and words of an angel instantly convey its meaning to others because this affects the language. A single sentence suffices to tell an attentive and wise angel what special apptitudes his counterpart possesses. A single word from an angel can encompass more than any number of words by a person. According to Swedenborg, angels also have their own writing. This, too, is utterly unique and corresponds to the degree of wisdom and understanding of the angel concerned. For people, it is illegible.

According to Swedenborg, the souls of the deceased will be welcomed into Heaven by the angels, who protect and care for them.

Divine marriages

By Swedenborg's view, the exterior of an angel—its raiment, dwelling, language, and writing—is a reflection of its inner nature.

Contrary to the ideas of many Christian denominations and theologians (according to whom angels do not have sex), Swedenborg says that sex really does take place between angels and it mirrors their previous human existence. Marriages also take place in Heaven; in fact, in a certain sense they are even essential, since a man and a woman can never be complete in himself or herself. However, if their souls conflate, they will then become a single, sexless angel rather than remaining a pair of spirits. But these fusions can only take place with divine approval.

For Swedenborg, all this takes place in a world without time, and the angels also have no consciousness of time. The sole aim of angelic development is godliness, although they can never attain this. According to Swedenborg, all power comes from God, and only God is infinite and perfect.

If approved, a male and female angel can coalesce with one another and become a sexless angel.

The work of angels, undertaken in their heavenly form, mainly consists in protecting people.

OPUS ANGELORUM

Opus Angelorum, founded as *Engelwerk* (the work of angels) and also called the Confraternity of the Guardian Angels, is a fundamentalist Catholic organization, which is also highly controversial within the Church. This charismatic community has tasked itself with tightening the bond between people and angels. It was founded by Gabriele Bitterlich (1896–1978), who is known within today's Engelwerk as the "Mother." This Austrian woman was a simple housewife who saw her guardian angel for the first time when she was just four years old, and in the last thirty years of her life

experienced and transcribed repeated revelations. She ultimately produced over 80,000 handwritten pages, including detailed notes on angels and demons. Bitterlich listed the names of over 400 angels and 200 demons, along with information about these spirits.

Marriage with an angel

Engelwerk members must achieve various levels of consecration in order to penetrate the inner circle of the angel world. Opus Angelorum is entered through the Consecration to the Guardian Angel ceremony, which gives "to our holy guardian angels all power over us, and solemnly binds us to them." This is a holy contract. With the later Consecration to All Angels the members are mystically married with an angel, and beyond this there is another three-stage Consecration of Reparation. Anyone who undergoes these is inducted by the holy angels into the ranks of guardian angels and enjoys a right to the same degree of special intercession with God as the guardian angels.

In 1992, the Catholic Congregation of the Faithful forbade some of the central rites and teachings of the Consecration to All Angels. Since then, Bitterlich's revelations, and the names of the angels she listed, may no longer be disseminated in the Catholic Church. The son of the founder, Father Hansjörg Bitterlich, stated that Engelwerk was destroyed by this decree. In some dioceses, priests who belong to Engelwerk are even forbidden to preach.

But in the year 2000 a new prayer was approved for the Consecration to the Guardian Angels, which may also be disseminated officially.

For Gabriele Bitterlich, it was important not only to disseminate knowledge about the angels, but especially to create strong relationships between individual people and their guardian angels, taking the following Biblical verse as her lead: "Are they not all ministering spirits sent forth to serve, for the sake of those who are to attain salvation?" (Hebrews 1:14)

The present as the Biblical end time

One of the many criticisms of Opus Angelorum is that angels are at the center of its teachings, instead of God and Jesus Christ.

Engelwerk assumes that the Last Battle between the angels and demons will take place in the present—which Engelwerk adherents see as the Biblical end time. Humanity is a part of this battle, since each of us has bound ourselves to a good or evil spirit.

Engelwerk also justifies itself with a comment by Pope John Paul II on the topic of angels: "It is precisely the religious encounter with the world of the purely spiritual being that becomes valuable as a revelation of his own being, not only as body but also as spirit, and

of his belonging to a design of salvation that is truly great and efficacious within a community of personal beings who serve the providential design of God for man and with man."

The official arm of Engelwerk is the Order of the Regular Canons of the Holy Cross, which was revived in 1976. This order supervises the entire membership and organization of Engelwerk on behalf of the Vatican. Today, it numbers approximately 140 members at twelve locations.

Engelwerk attaches particular importance to the fact that every mortal develops a close relationship with his or her guardian angel.

According to tradition, God revealed the Koran to the prophet Mohammed during a battle.

ANGELS IN ISLAM

Angels also play an important role in Islam, the third great monotheistic religion (one that recognizes a single God). They are part of the statement of faith recited by every Muslim and, in the form of the Archangel Jibril (Gabriel), in a certain way even participated in the founding of Islam itself.

Islam (Arabic for "submission to God") is the second largest world religion after Christianity. The Koran and the Sunnah are, for approximately 1.2 billion devotees, the most important works of the faith. While the Sunnah contains the collected words and actions of

the prophet Mohammed, according to the Islamic faith the Koran is the literal revelation of Allah to Mohammed ("praised one, worthy of praise"). He was probably born in 570 in Mecca, and died in 632 in Medina. Since he is viewed as the last and most important prophet, he also bears the title "The Seal of the Prophets."

Gabriel and Mohammed

But the most important year in Islam in terms of angels is 610, when the Archangel Jibril is said to have appeared to Mohammed. Jibril communicated the first verses of the Koran to the prophet then; the remaining verses were revealed to Mohammed over the next twenty-three years. By his own account, Mohammed also learned the motions of the Muslim prayer ritual by watching the angels at worship.

Another meeting of the Archangel Gabriel with Mohammed, described by the Persian scholar Al-Bukhari in the collections of Hadith, or honored traditions based on the life of Mohammed, sheds light on the prohibition of alcohol in Islam: "(That night) I was given two cups; one full of milk and the other full of wine. I was asked to take either of them which I liked, and I took the milk and drank it. On that it was said to me, 'You have taken the right path (religion). If you had taken the wine, your (Muslim) nation would have gone astray'."

In the *Hadith Gabriel* narrative, the additional pillars of Islam are described in the form of a discussion between Mohammed and the Archangel Gabriel, who is in disguise.

Emergence and tasks of the angels

According to the mystic traditions of Islam and Sufism, angels—called *al-mala'ik* in Arabic—were created by Allah on the first day, so that they should glorify him. But the glorification of Allah is not the only duty of these bright spirits which, according to Islam, can take on a variety of physical forms and may thus have differing numbers of wings. The *mala'ik* are beings as formidable as they are powerful, who also had the task of conveying divine messages to the prophet. In

Angels accompany Mohammed's ascent into Heaven.

The Koran (here a richly decorated manuscript from the eighteenth century) also recognizes angels.

addition, they intercede for people and provide pragmatic aid. After death, they remain at the side of people who have died and accompany them on the way to Paradise. But they are also active as prosecutors before judges, since they know all human deeds.

Another Hadith says that 120 days after every human conception, Allah sends a *mala'ik* who has various tasks with respect to the unborn child:

"(The matter of the Creation of) a human being is put together in the womb of the mother in forty days, and then he becomes a clot of thick blood for a similar period, and then a piece of flesh for a similar period. Then Allah sends an angel who is ordered to write four things. He is ordered to write down his [i.e. the new creature's] deeds, his livelihood, his (date of) death, and whether he will be blessed or wretched (in religion). Then the soul is breathed into him." (Sahih Al-Bukhari No. 4430)

Angels and unborn humans

Belief in Allah's *mala'ik* remains an important component of Islam today. The deeds of the *mala'ik* are described in many of the 114 surah (chapters) of the Koran, and they are included in the articles of faith fundamental to the belief of every Muslim.

In Islam there are six articles of faith. These are: faith in God, in his angels, in his revelations (i.e. the holy books), in his messengers (meaning the prophets of God, which include Abraham, Moses, Jesus, and naturally Mohammed), in the Last Judgment and life after death, and in Allah's divine plan.

Similar to Christianity, Islam embraces the concept of a Paradise and a Hell, into which humans are received after death in accordance with their acts on Earth.

Islam also recognizes the three Archangels of the Judaeo-Christian teachings: Michael (Mika'al), Gabriel (Jibril), and Lucifer (Iblis). The Devil was once a good angel, who refused to honor Adam and was therefore driven out of Paradise. In his own defense, Iblis argued that he was created from fire and Adam was only made of clay. Shaitaan is the name by which he is known as a fallen angel.

The post-death examination

There are additional Archangels that are only mentioned in Islam. The Archangel Israfil will blow his horn on the Day of Judgment to give the signal for the resurrection of the dead. Izra'il—also Azrael or Azra'il—is the designated angel of death (see box, page 48). Forty days after death, these angels awaken the deceased. Only after this does the task of the Archangels Munkar and Nakir begin. These two appear to the deceased in their graves and examine whether they are firm in the faith—and if they find that this is not the case, they exact punishment.

The Hadith states that *mala'ik* do not enter any dwelling that contains an image or sculpture of a person, a dog, or any other animal. The following statement is also part of the Hadith: "When Allah's

The jinn
Jinn also appear in the Koran. These are non-human spirits, and according to surah 72, there are three kinds of them: malicious demons that may be dangerous to people, hermaphrodite spirits that live alongside humankind on Earth, and human *doppelgangers*. Thus jinn live neither in Paradise nor in the fires of Hell, but here on Earth. The Koran therefore also applies to them, and they may be both good and bad. One of these, according to Islamic doctrine, is Iblis, the Devil, who is also a jinni (see page 67).

Non-Christian art also represents angels: here the emperor Farrukhsiyar is encircled by heavenly spirits and birds of paradise.

An angel follows the prophet Mohammed as he rides.

servant has read the Koran all the way through once, 60,000 angels pray for him."

Spirits of smokeless fire

Contrary to the *al-mala'ik*, jinn were created from "smokeless fire" (surah 15.27), rather than light. As a result, fire flows in their veins instead of blood. These spirits can be conjured up by reciting specific verses of the Koran. However, since this procedure is very painful for the jinn, they are not disposed to be friendly when they have been thus summoned. In any case, such summons are forbidden in Islam.

Muslims distinguish two groups of jinn: the Islamic and the non-Islamic. The difference between them is believed to have resulted from the following events:

At a meeting once, several of the jinn noticed that they could not hear the angels speaking. While seeking to understand the reason for this, they met the prophet Mohammed, who read the Koran to them. As a result, they professed their faith in Islam. The remaining jinn—who were not present at the time—can freely select which religion they belong to.

There five jinn classes in total: marit, ifrit, sheitan, gillan, and jann. The mightiest, proudest, and most arrogant are marit. Their skin is blue or green, and their hair is always wet. The *ifrit* (Arabic for "dust") are considered the next most powerful (27th surah, verse 39). Although one surah describes ifrit as demons of the underworld with horns, lions' claws, and donkeys' hooves, they are nevertheless often illustrated as strong young men. These include the spirit of vengeance, who carries out the punishment of sinners.

ANGELS IN THE KABBALAH

Kabbalah, the secret mystic teachings of Judaism, have enjoyed several years of increased interest and justifiable popularity. Singers such as Madonna and Britney Spears, actresses including Winona Ryder and Gwyneth Paltrow, and other stars, like David Beckham and Paris Hilton, are well-known adherents—albeit to a contemporary version described pejoratively by its critics as "McMysticism."

The Tree of Life, which shows the ten sephiroth with twenty-two connecting paths, is the core of the Kabbalah.

A special attraction of the Kabbalah seems to reside in the fact that a practical Kabbalah exists alongside the theoretical one: magic. Kabbalah is a complicated belief structure that in a number of respects is based on a kind of number magic. Numbers are also of central importance in Jewish mysticism with respect to the role of angels.

The Sephiroth

An important basic principle of the Kabbalah is that it should not only be studied in depth, but also experienced. The relationship between masters and students is therefore particularly important in these esoteric teachings.

The late thirteenth century *Zohar* (Hebrew, "The Glossator's Book"), by the Spaniard Mosche de Leon, is considered the most important Kabbalistic writing. Next to the Tanach and the Talmud it is the most important work in Judaism.

But the core work for information on the role of angels in Kabbalism is *Sefer Yetzirah* (Hebrew for "Book of Creation"). This is the oldest surviving text of esoteric teachings and is supposed to have been written by Abraham, the ancestor of Israel. It contains, among other things, ten *sephiroth* (enumerations) and the twenty-two letters of the Hebrew alphabet, which have a central meaning for all esoteric teachings. The book set out the connections between the numbers and the letters, and their significance for the path to enlightenment. Astonishingly, despite its enormous significance for the esoteric teachings, *Sefer Yetzirah* is very short—fewer than two hundred words long.

The Tree of Life (or *Ez Chajim*), which shows the ten sephiroth (numbers) and their twenty-two connecting paths (letters), is at the center of the Kabbalah. But sephiroth is also the name for the ten divine emanations (projected radiances), which together—in the symbolic sense—make up the "heavenly (or primordial) man," who is known as Adam Kadmon. Earth man is the image of this primordial man but lacks his three special attributes of wisdom, glory, and

The Kabbalah is intended to be both studied and experienced.

immortality. In addition, one guardian angel and three angel princes are assigned to each Sephirah. In accordance with the ten holy names of God there are ten Archangels: Metatron, Rasiel, Tafkiel, Zadkiel, Chamael, Michael, Haniel, Raphael, Gabriel, and Sandalphon. Theoretical Kabbalists meditate on the Tree of Life, while it serves practical magicians as a model for their activities.

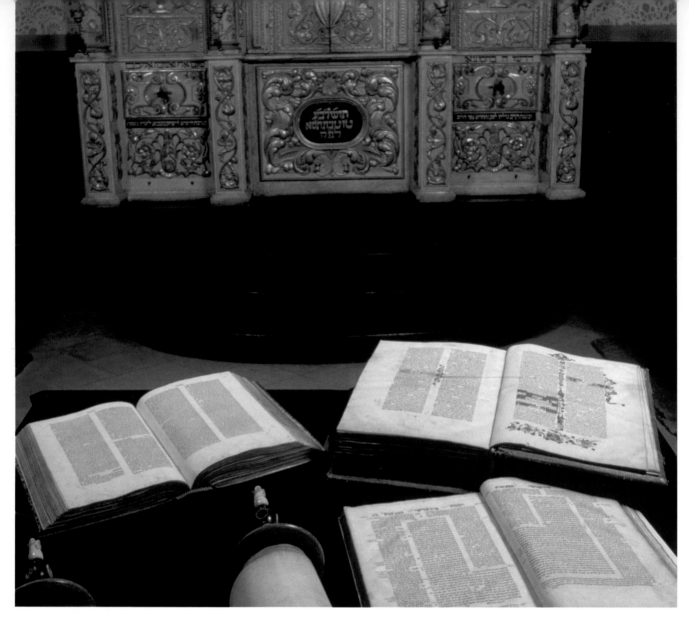

In the Jewish faith, angels reside in three of seven spheres. There are over three billion angels.

301,655,722 angels in three spheres

The Jewish perspective on the world of angels is similar to the Christian one, although the Kabbalistic view differs substantially in some respects. The Kabbalah presents itself as a guide to the path that leads to God. With the assistance of the angels, it leads through various heavenly halls—by means of the tree of the angels (the Tree of Life, in relation to the angels), the performance of rituals, the invocation of angel names, and the use of special words—to the overcoming of demons. Because the goal of all human efforts is ever-greater self-perfection in order to become Adam Kadmon and in order to recreate the original heavenly state.

The Kabbalah mentions 301,655,722 angels, who are found in three of the seven spheres of existence: the sphere of the Gods and highest forces, the sphere of the angels and Seraphim, the sphere of the angels and Genii, the sphere of men, the sphere of the animal kingdom, the sphere of the vegetable kingdom, and the sphere of minerals and elements. In addition to these, there are four further worlds that are mutually interpenetrative with the spheres. *Aziluth* is the pure and immaculate creation of God. *Beriah* is the purely spiritual world of the highest angelic beings. *Yetzirah* is the intermediate world, and *Assia* is the visible creation.

Opposite page: The Kabbalah is all the rage—literature on the topic currently sells very well.

The 72-character name of God

Along with the Archangels and other choirs, a further seventy-two holy angels are named, the Genii. In nine groups of eight angels, each one of them bears another name of God. Together they form the 72-character name of God (Hebrew *Shem Ha-Mephoresh*). Their names are formed from verses 19–21 of the second Book of Moses (Exodus 14:19–21). These must be written one under the other (and only verse 20 backwards), and then read perpendicularly. A masculine (*al*) or feminine (*ah*) ending is attached to the three letters, so that all these names have five letters in the source language. The complex Kabbalistic angel system embraces an additional 360 angel chiefs and ten core adversaries (including Lilith and Samael), who oppose the Archangels.

The angel hierarchy in the Kabbalistic Tree of Life

Realm (And Translation)	Corresponding Choir	Archangels
1. Kether (crown)	Seraphim	Metatron
2. Chokmah (wisdom)	Cherubim	Rasiel
3. Binah (intelligence)	Thrones	Tzafkiel
4. Chesed (love)	Dominions	Zadkiel
5. Geburah (severity)	Virtues	Chamael
6. Tiphereth (beauty)	Powers	Raphael
7. Netzach (victory)	Principalities	Haniel
8. Hod (majesty)	Archangels	Michael
9. Yesod (foundation)	Angels	Gabriel
10. Malkuth (kingdom)	Humanity	Sandalfon

ANGELS IN ANTHROPOSOPHY

The Austrian pedagogue, philosopher, and esoteric Rudolf Steiner (1861–1925) was not only the founder of biodynamic agriculture and the Rudolf Steiner (Waldorf) Schools, but also the spiritual philosophy of anthroposophy. Anthroposophy understands the universe as the manifestation of the divine, which is in constant evolution. At the end of this process stands the overcoming of all material obstacles and a return to divine origins.

The framework of anthroposophical beliefs is a combination of the ideas of Christianity with Eastern teachings. By means of explanation of the name, Steiner wrote: "Now, whereas that which people can know about themselves through their senses and through the understanding gained through observation of the world can be called "anthropology," then what the 'inner man' or 'spiritual man' can know may be called "anthroposophy." Anthroposophy is thus the knowledge of the spiritual being; and this knowledge pertains not only to humanity, but is a knowledge of everything that the spiritual human being can perceive in the spiritual world, in the same way that the sensory human being can perceive the sensible world."

The human being as a compound entity

Anthroposophy sees humans as compound beings. They consist of four intertwining levels: the physical body, the etheric body, the astral body, and the ego or "I."

Angels play an important role in anthroposophy. Rudolf Steiner wrote and gave two lectures that discuss them: *Spiritual Hierarchies* and *The Spiritual Beings in Celestial Bodies and the Realms of Nature*. Even as early as the age of eight, Steiner himself is said to have experienced extrasensory perceptions of other worlds and spirits.

According to Steiner, angels are spiritual entities that remain invisible to most people, although they are recognizable by the spiritually aware.

The foundation for the organization of the material and spiritual worlds is Steiner's hierarchy. In ascending order, he identifies the mineral world, the vegetable world, the animal world, the human world and, above it, the world of invisible beings:

"Through awareness of extrasensory perceptions … it is possible for humans to ascend a distance to those virtues and entities that constitute the continuation of the four-fold progression present within the Earth in the extrasensory, invisible world."

The realm of invisible entities

Rudolf Steiner understood the elemental spirits of earth, water, air, and fire, which are "spellbound within all things," as the lowest level of the invisible world. Everything around us we owe to these elemental spirits. Through them, the plants grow, water moves through its cycle of precipitation and evaporation, and

Rudolf Steiner, the founder of anthroposophy.

Elemental spirits form the lowest stage of the invisible world—above
them are, among other things, the Angels and Archangels.

the wind blows. Above these elemental spirits are
the higher spirits, the angels (*angelos*, also guardian
angels), followed by the Archangels (*archangeloi*). Still
further up in the hierarchy are the Principalities
(*archai*, spirits of the age) who are also supposed to
have once lived as human beings. This first of three
angel hierarchies is associated with the Holy Spirit
in anthroposophy.

Angels of the present age

Archai, which are elemental forces and spirits of the age, have a special role. They are responsible for the relationship of all mankind with the Earth. Rudolf Steiner also presents the concept that specific angels are responsible for entire epochs. The angel of our time, for example, is Michael.

Archangeloi, called the sons of fire, must answer for the development of the collective souls of entire races and civilizations, as well as the relationship of these group souls with those of each individual person.

Angelos are concerned with individual humans. Their influence is greatest during our childhood; later we develop individually, in accordance with our own desires. In old age, angelos try to help people regain the spirituality they may have drifted away from.

In contrast to the angel hierarchy laid out by Dionysius the Areopagite (see page 38 ff), Rudolf Steiner's second hierarchy follows with the spirits of form: Dominions (*Kyriotetes*, world leaders), Virtues (*Dynameis*, world forces), and Powers (*Exusiai*, visible ones). Each higher angel choir represents a higher stage of evolution. This second hierarchy is assigned to the Son—Jesus Christ.

In anthroposophy, Michael is seen as the angel of our time.

Luciferian and Arihmanian forces fight over humans. Here, Michael and Satan struggle over the body of Moses.

Angels have the greatest influence on humans during childhood. With increasing age, people become more independent.

Luciferian and Ahrimanian forces

In the highest hierarchy, which belongs to God, the Seraphim, Cherubim, and Thrones are to be found. According to Steiner, the duties of these wise and inexpressibly wonderful angels cannot be expressed in human language. According to the anthroposophical model, humankind itself will one day become the tenth hierarchy.

In addition to the elemental spirits and angels there are two forces, neither good nor evil, that have an influence on people. The Luciferian forces are described as hedonistic and worldly. They attempt to make humans fulfill themselves without restraint in the spiritual realm. The Ahrimanians, forces of cold intelligence, counteract their efforts. They want humans to ground themselves utterly in their physical plane, so that their worldview is purely material and technical.

With Christ's assistance, it is the individual's job to hold these two forces in balance. Both forces have their qualities. Ideally, the result is personal spiritual development in relation to one's fellow human beings and the life around us.

The existence of angels remains a matter of faith.

CONCLUSION

Although the traditional Christian concept of angels took precedence in this book, less known concepts of the divine realm also found a place in it. Nevertheless only a fraction of the knowledge currently circulating about angels could be presented here. Among the esoteric and New Age movements, especially, which often combine elements from different religions, much has been written on angels as personal companions and teachers. Angel books, angel seminars, and angel congresses, as well as the idea that there are divine companions who can guide us along the way, are very popular in these circles.

The existence of angels cannot be proven in any scientific sense. They remain, even today, an article of faith—as do the different models of the divine world with its Archangels, participants in the divine plan, and their demonic adversaries.

But even if theology and the natural sciences have bid adieu to them, the angels have not—on the

Are angels divine spirits—or perhaps visitors from outer space, as some people believe?

whole—said goodbye to people. That new theories continually emerge in the pseudoscientific disciplines is just one indication of this.

Angels as extraterrestrials

Erich von Däniken (born 1935), a Swiss author, assumed that anything concerning angels actually represented extraterrestrial visitors, who came to the Earth long ago. His books are extremely popular and have sold by the million in over thirty languages. His connection of UFOs and belief in angels seems to have struck a nerve with the public, even though his theories are not taken seriously by scientists.

However, the publications of the British biologist Rupert Sheldrake (born 1942), whose work connects natural science and angel teachings, are another matter. According to Sheldrake, complex activity structures are not only present in all organisms but also in everything else—which only seems not to be alive, such as rock, for example. He calls these "morphogenetic fields." They have consciousness and memory and, in addition, they still promote the development of the universe. That is, they take on the precise role that is attributed to angels in Judaism, Islam and Christianity.

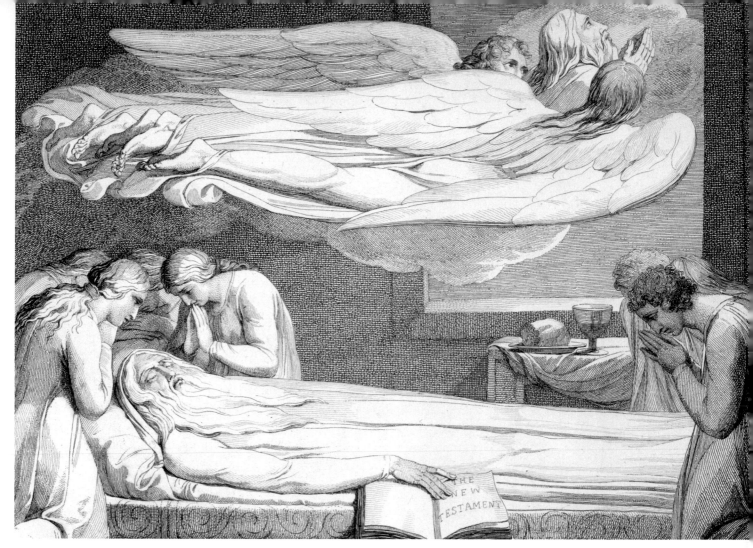

Many people who have near-death experiences tell of light or spirit beings who welcomed them or sent them back to their life on Earth.

Near-death experiences

In another scientific field, gerontology, so-called near-death experiences have involved angels so often that the pre-occupation with angels has been rekindled. One speaks of a near-death experience when a person has been clinically dead for a limited time and, when revived, reports seeing or experiencing things during that time. Due to advances in medical equipment, cases such as this happen far more often today than in the past.

Some patients who have near-death experiences describe a bright light, and beings of light or spirits, who appeared around them to escort them into another world, but then sent them back to their lives, as their time has not yet come. Some tell of an incredible happiness and contentment they experienced when meeting these spirits. Other patients tell of

veritably hellish journeys during which they encountered demons. It seems natural to draw connections between these kinds of reports and the familiar concepts of Heaven and Hell. The works of Raymond A. Moody and Elisabeth Kübler-Ross have generated a great deal of attention in this field. The issue of whether these experiences are born of drug-induced hallucinations or whether they are genuine experiences indicative of another world, and life after death, is much debated.

Nonetheless, the idea that spiritual beings do exist is ubiquitous, found in a large number of religions and faith communities, and the various concepts of angels exhibit amazing parallels despite all their differences. These are reason enough to at least accept the possibility that there may be a spiritual level apart from the mundane physical world—a realm in which spirits such as angels could exist.

Sources

Aquinas, St Thomas. *Summa Theologica*. Trans. Fathers of the English Dominican Province. Christian Classics, New Ed ed., 1981.

Benedikt, Heinrich Elijah. *Die Kabbala*. Freiburg, 2000.

Berger, Peter L. *A Rumor of Angels; Modern Society and the Rediscovery of the Supernatural*. Garden City, NY: Doubeday, 1969.

The Bible. Revised Standard Version.

Davidson, Gustav. *A Dictionary of Angels*. New York, 1971.

Dieckmann, Dorothea. *Wie Engel erscheinen*. Munich, 1995.

Dion, Fortune. *The Mystical Qabalah*, revised ed. York Beach, ME: Samuel Weiser, 2000.

Giovetti, Paola. *Angels: The Role of Celestial Guardians and Beings of Light*. Trans. Toby McCormick. York Beach, ME: Samuel Weiser, 1993.

Godwin, Malcolm. *Angels: An Endangered Species*. New York: Simon and Schuster, 1990.

Komroff, Manuel, ed. *The Apocrypha or Non-Canonical Books of the Bible*. New York: Arno Press, 1972.

Krauss, Heinrich. *Die Engel. Überlieferung. Gestalt, Deutung*. Munich, 2000.

Krauss, Heinrich. *Kleines Lexikon der Engel*. Von Ariel bis Zebaoth. Munich, 2001.

Kriele, Alexa. *Wie im Himmel so auf Erden. Christliche Engelkunde*. Munich: Ullstein, 2004.

Llewellyn, Claire. *Saints and Angels*. Boston: Kingfisher, 2003.

MacLean, Dorothy. *To Hear the Angels Sing*. Findhorn, 1980.

Schipperges, Heinrich. *Die Welt der Engel bei Hildegard von Bingen*. Freiburg: Herder, 1995.

Schröder, Hans-Werner. *L'Homme et les Anges*. Franchesse: Editions Iona, 1995.

Steiner, Rudolf. *The Spiritual Hierarchies and the Physical World; Reality and Illusion*. Hudson, NY: Anthroposophic Press, 1996.

Swedenborg, Emanuel. *Heaven and Hell*. Trans. George F. Dole. New York: Pillar Books, 1976.

Swedenborg, Emanuel. *Life After Death*. New York: New Church Press, nd.

Vorgrimler, Herbert, Ursula Bernauer, Thomas Sternberg. *Engel. Erfahrungen göttlicher Nähe*. Freiburg, 2001.

Picture credits

Index